The
Chain

Also by Chimene Suleyman

The Good Immigrant USA (co-editor)

The
Chain

Love, Betrayal, and the
Sisterhood That Heals Us

Chimene
Suleyman

HARPER

An Imprint of HarperCollins*Publishers*

THE CHAIN. Copyright © 2024 by Chimene Suleyman. All rights reserved. Printed in the United States of America. No part of this book may be used or reproduced in any manner whatsoever without written permission except in the case of brief quotations embodied in critical articles and reviews. For information, address HarperCollins Publishers, 195 Broadway, New York, NY 10007.

HarperCollins books may be purchased for educational, business, or sales promotional use. For information, please email the Special Markets Department at SPsales@harpercollins.com.

Originally published in Great Britain in 2024 by Weidenfeld & Nicolson.

FIRST U.S. EDITION

Library of Congress Cataloging-in-Publication Data has been applied for.

ISBN 978-0-06-339295-3

24 25 26 27 28 LBC 5 4 3 2 1

To my *anne* and *baba*, thank you.

The
Chain

I think back to a time on a bright blue lake. Clear skies. The water just shallow enough to drown in. There were fourteen fish in a bucket of water, kept alive for longer so they may be fresher when dead. My love, is this not how men love women?

That is to say, you will kill us, then stand back and watch us remember how to breathe.

Oh, sinner man, where you gonna run
    to?
Sinner man where you gonna run to?
Where you gonna run to?
All on that day
                — *Sinner Man, African American*
                  traditional spiritual song

Shortly before the snow melted, there were no answers for questions no one had known to ask.

It was in a clinic in Queens. A metal detector securing the distance between us and the street, but nothing could narrow the space between actual refuge and the myth of it. From the outside it looked like the man was scrolling through photos on his phone, showing them to the woman beside him. From the outside he looked like a man who had taken days off work to care for her. From the outside, it was not possible to tell that we had shared a sandwich that morning, then driven the short distance from Brooklyn with the radio on. My partner showed me photographs of his father. A man whose cheekbones were cut the same, whose eyes were curved in a similar way. My partner joked about his father's many girlfriends, dozens and dozens of women all at once, he said. I looked at him, in that way a girlfriend does when she wants to ask her man if it is more than cheekbones that are cut from the same cloth.

He laughed. *One of you, my love, is more than enough.*

I have a clear memory of the dog that lingered beside the traffic lights on the way to the clinic. A huge white husky-mix with grey spots. I focused on the dog. Let its fur and open mouth become my only thought as we drove past it. Until it was a dog in the distance. Until it was a shape of white and grey. Until it didn't exist at all.

I thought about that dog as I filled in forms twenty minutes later. I think about that dog often. How it was there one minute and gone the next. How it was in the window, then the side mirror, then on a street in Queens I was no longer on. I play an alternative version of it in my mind – of stopping the car and getting out at the traffic lights, of following the dog to its home, keeping it somewhere in my eyeline. I had wanted to keep looking at it, wanted to stop a minute, or twenty minutes, or more, longer at those traffic lights and not go beyond them. I thought about the dog as the receptionist called my name.

He did not accompany me into the consulting room. And as a practitioner squeezed gel onto my stomach, I felt a foreign and illegible agitation rise. She asked if I wanted to look at the screen. I told her I didn't. I hadn't wanted to see the black and white of it all, the outline, a head-shape, a movement: was that a hand, a foot, a heart, my heart, that I would not see again?

★

Four days earlier I stood at my window. It was snowing, but not in that way you should find romantic. Rather, it settled on parked cars and the pavement, oppressive in its thickness, aggressive as it fell diagonally and cut the sky.

My partner's mother had been sick for some weeks. He had flown regularly to Atlanta to be with her in hospital, taking red-eye flights back to New York on the days that he could, frequently arriving at my apartment sometime before morning turned to midday.

Often he was tired, and spoke of having slept in hospital chairs until the nurses made him leave, staying briefly in his mother's empty house before returning to be with her.

How can we be parents right now, when I'm losing one? he'd say, cross-legged on my rug in the living room, folding and unfolding laundry, rolling his sweaters precisely and placing them into an overnight bag. Weeks passed like this: I was pregnant and couldn't stand the smell of chicken; he was distracted and drank cinnamon tea with me on the days he was in Brooklyn. On that night, as it snowed, his phone rang to voice-mail, and the white outside suffocated me, snared me in a space, a life I wanted to split open, that snow, that fucking snow that kept me in place. And in the morning his message came, that his mother was dead, gone, and I lay in bed, face down on my stomach, as though choking on mouthfuls of snow, that fucking snow, shovelled into my throat.

★

I did not want an abortion. Nor did I want a child. Such is the complexity of a person who lives alongside assigned roles. I was ruled by fear – the dread of not keeping it, the dread of becoming a mother. There was no part of me that aligned, nor would there be fully again. My body had gone into the action of protecting what was two months within it. Because women's bodies are not singular, yet I had further understood the meaning of being treated as mass on this day. To be a woman in the London of my youth was to be an idea before human. And so our bodies were touched and stroked and grabbed in bars and on roads. We were told who to be and how to be it. To be a woman was to be a shape, smell, size; a walk, then a dress style, a mother, a mother one day, and so on.

But we were there: a clinic in Queens, finality around us. The doctor, a woman with short-cropped hair, spoke to me with the patience of a person who had said these same words a thousand times. The first pill, she explained, would terminate the pregnancy. For twenty-four hours I would carry it as such, lifeless, until it passed from me. She asked if I was sure, and in the absence of knowing how to say no, I nodded. She asked if I was alone, a question now peculiar for its answer. No, I told her, my partner was in the waiting room, and what had taken us there would surely remove us from it. I walked the staircase to the waiting area. White walls. I read the messages on my phone – of how we'd get through this, that we'd be home soon, eat ice cream and watch re-runs of shows – that he had only gone to find the restroom, and I should stay for him near the receptionist and wait.

In a chair facing her desk, my winter coat lay across my lap, and I thought of the dog. How I had turned to watch it through the rear window, until it was a hound in the background, until it was an outline of ashen silver. How it was right there until, when all was said and done, it wasn't. And I scanned the room until I saw it, the restroom, the door wide open and no one inside. As the waiting room emptied, as a young woman tapped the keyboard of her computer with perfectly pointed nails, what I understood came only as sound, or half of one, escaped from somewhere inside my mouth until it had nowhere left to go. He was gone. He was gone and my calls went only to voicemail.

Outside the clinic I howled. Walking quickly, circling the block as though searching, when there was no one and nothing left to look for. I was both frantic and insensible, both numb and wild. If I found him this would all be over, if I found him every question I had not previously known to ask would be answered.

I remember dropping, slipping in the sludge, sitting on my knees in the snow that was partially brown. I screamed again. And then, somehow, I was at the subway, had climbed the stairs to the platform. What if he were dead. What if he were on the tracks or fallen from a bridge. But the trains were still running, and the stations came, 21 Street, Greenpoint, Nassau, and I texted his friend as they passed.

You may remember me, I wrote, telling him all that had just happened, without knowing myself.

Where are you? the friend replied. *Are you okay? How did he seem?*

8

I cannot recall my answers. They do not matter. After how long, I don't know, I was at my apartment. Time is an illusion when there is no reason left to count it. But it was outside my home that I saw the messages from him.

Do not reach out to my friends again. You are ruined. There is nothing good or human about you. You are not someone anyone should ever be with. No one should love you.

No one should love me.

I reached for my keys, then put them away. I turned the handle on my apartment door and expected, rightly, that it would open. The shirts he left in my closet were no longer there. His T-shirts that had filled the bottom drawer, gone. His sneakers that had formed a neat line against my shoes, and some of my belongings too, gone with him.

No one should love me. And I believed him. Because I had been taught to.

★

In the days that followed I asked the superintendent to show me the security footage of the hallway outside my apartment. I checked the time on the recording. When I had been with the doctor, he had climbed the stairs to my home and entered with a spare key. On the screen I watched him carry his shirts to the waste disposal room, then dump them in the garbage chute. On the screen I watched him reappear with more of his belongings and throw those too, before leaving with a small red painting of his, and a bag full of his things, and some of mine. This is what it felt to be haunted. To see precisely without any doubt, or alternative, the moment someone set about to break your life, to invade your home, and above all else present safety as little more than an illusion. There was no question over whether he had been nervous, scared or panicked. He wasn't. And any desire I had to imagine a man who ran from the clinic, or my apartment, with pain, or guilt, or a breakdown induced by the hours that had happened before this, was replaced by the clear vision of a man entirely calm, entirely poised, entirely in control.

On the road outside the clinic, I had screamed. Whatever decision I had made in that place no longer felt like mine. He was dead inside me. The sky collapsed. I had only the security footage – I watched him, again and again, take his things and dispose of them as though he had murdered himself, then set about cleaning the crime scene.

In seven months' time I would wonder who my pregnancy could have been. Both of them now a fantasy, neither fully mine nor real. He stole the sky. How do you ever forgive someone for taking that.

i.

The village is always on fire.
Men stay away from the kitchens,
take up in outhouses with concrete
    floors,
while the women — soot in their hair —
initiate the flames into their small
    routines.

                 — *Sophie Collins, 'untitled'*

That *he* was gone should not have been a surprise. He was always gone in some capacity or another. That began very early on when he prepared me for, as he described it, his mental disabilities. His high-functioning autism, he said, came with agoraphobia and it was hard for him to commit to the things we had planned. Nights out, if they happened at all, quickly turned into nights at home. My home. And it seemed we were always up against something. Losing jobs and moving house; delays on the subway and his mother's poor health; his father's recurring absence and his sister's rape, and his ex-girlfriend's death, and my ex-partner's thoughtless ways, a cancelled flight, a bus stuck in traffic, and the lost equipment on a film shoot he had worked on, and wasn't the world spinning in another direction from us, and a deadline that had been pushed, and when the core of a star runs out of hydrogen fuel it will implode under the weight of gravity, and a lost phone, and *Fleetwood Mac wrote the* Rumours *album during their most destructive heartbreak*, and an eye infection that takes weeks to heal, and *'The Chain' is truly the most sensational song by Fleetwood Mac, perhaps in the world*, but he was funny, and I had my words, and wasn't that lucky seeing as he was a comedian, and I – what was I? – *could our love really be the only thing keeping him alive?*, and several billion years after its life starts, a star will die; how the star dies, however, depends on what type of star it is.

★

New York smells of sewage in the summer. Manhattan in particular. It has a kind of decomposing stink, like flesh, and condensation drips onto your head from air conditioners hooked up in half-open windows. The cockroaches and rats held court around the bins, the half drank coffee cups and mustard-covered napkins brimming over. I liked the rats. They were fearless and smart in a way I thought you needed to be to live in that city. They cotched near your sandals while you waited for the bus or smoked a cigarette away from the outdoor area of a bar or restaurant. And just as quickly, you learned the IKEA boat from Pier 11 dropped you at Red Hook for the best free views, that everyone had their own theory on where '86'd from a bar' came from, that if you want an uptown train, you entered the subway the same side the cars drove uptown on, that if you ought to call an ambulance, order an Uber instead.

I was new to the city, new to a country I had only seen tower above me on cinema screens. Newly single, straight from a relationship with a man who had spent years lying, then lying more to cover the pretence of it all. I had few friends, and they too were new. What do people do when everything is fresh, peculiar, when the newest of all is to feel wholly alone? Try dating apps, I suppose. Above anything, seek connection.

But any woman who has spent long enough in a bar, or a street, on a train, in an office, just existing, will tell you that men can be pushy, sex-crazed, confrontational, that they can't – no, won't – take a hint. Go online and the screen, the sense of pseudo-anonymity, aggravates that. There are the men whose response to 'hi! how r u?' is 'would love to smash / you look great I wanna bend you over / I want to put my cock between your tits / I'm good but would be better with you on my face / would love to make you squirt if the connection is right'. There are the guys who press you to meet at their house, or yours, for a first date, with no concept of safety or boundaries, or with a purposeful disregard for both. Those who send pictures of their dick, and ask for naked pictures of you. Then there are the racists. The ones who ask the brown girls if they're hairy, who tell the East Asian girls they love how doll-like and submissive they are, who ignore the Black women altogether, who tell Jewish women they are cheap dates and their noses are surprisingly small. The guys who write to say you have a nice face but should lose the weight, you have a nice arse in that dress in the photo but should wear less make-up, you have pretty hair but should smile in your pictures more. And the guys who descend into thirty-six angry messages, one after the other, because you didn't respond during the first hour. Or the men who don't reply for days having messaged twelve other women at once, devoted to sharing the poetry of 'hey wassup'. At best are the men with shit chat: 'hi' – 'hey' – 'you good?' – 'yeah how r u?' – 'good thanks, u?' – 'not bad, u?' – 'yeah, alright thanks, u?'

Often, the men I've liked and connected the best with in this world are not the ones I'd even consider on a dating app. The reverse must also be said.

When I matched with *him* our conversation was enjoyable. Consistent but not overblown, questions were asked and answered equally. The messages teemed with sarcasm which appealed entirely to my British sense of humour (and was otherwise deeply lacking in my experience of America). We messaged for a few weeks, then finally agreed to meet.

Remember, I was new to New York in those days. And watching a city in the movies is not research for living in one – I had not yet learned that in reality it was unedited and unvarnished. The unceasing sound of sirens. The roaches that gathered in apartment block hallways. People jammed in the subway either side of a deserted carriage, empty with the exception of blood or shit on the floor and seats. The men and women who screamed on subway platforms, who fought sometimes with passengers, often with the empty space in front of us all. Our phones pinged to warn us when a person with an axe or gun was just a few blocks away. During the summer months the notifications for shootouts were regular. On the more sweltering days you could feel it in the sky before it happened, the tension as tangible as the airless humidity. The bricks through windows of bars that had you flat out across the floor, glass splinters across your legs and back, the girl bleeding from her head on the ground next to you. Men pulled weapons on you when you rejected them. People you knew and loved were murdered. Shot in the head for chatting to the wrong girl outside your laundromat. Outside your local. But even so, it was the owner's elderly dead dog the community held candlelit vigils for instead of the person. Surviving New York violence was its own kind of souvenir. There was a pride in how much of this shit you were supposed to withstand.

That summer – the summer of 2016 – had been a particularly blistering one, and I wasn't too familiar with the kind of Manhattan bars where you dropped the name of someone who knew someone to get in. I ordered a drink. And I heard him say, *Turn around.* I did. He laughed. I think I must have done the same. His face partially veiled by the beard he kept in those early months. He said it felt like we already knew each other – then he threw in the word 'forever'. What a strange word. There's no such thing. Unless we existed elsewhere – in a parallel place, in an absence of reality.

His friend was DJing; R&B, soul, the popular songs that played New York that summer, the kind of music people found easy to move to. A couple of other guys he knew stood by the booth and danced, and we moved between speaking with them and talking alone, outside smoking cigarettes in the humidity that cloaks New York at night, his Marlboro Reds tucked into the rolled-up sleeve of his T-shirt. The conversation was as easy, as pleasing, as it had been online.

He flirted but kept it simple, briefly touching my arm, the occasional flattering remark, just enough eye contact. His friends were going to another bar on the edge of Chinatown under Manhattan Bridge, he said, and did I want to come. Outside, leaning against the dark green tiles, he asked if he could kiss me, the bridge's steel towers, the Q train clanking above. And when it was time to leave, with the same graciousness, he asked if he could order my Uber home, and pay for it.

We met again. A week later in a bar on the Lower East Side, the same friend of his DJed as we shared tortilla chips at the bar, bonded over the particulars of my routines, the quirks and peculiarities we seemed to share so many of, as he mirrored what mattered to me.

We met again. A bar in the East Village I had been to before and chosen for us. He was affectionate and polite, the bartenders laughed with him and responded with warmth to his being there.

We met again. A comedy night in a basement bar he was performing at. I felt trusted, involved, he was vulnerable and I was in on it.

Then, later that evening, someone he knew referred to me as *his* girl.

This was rare for New York, perhaps for a lot of cities, but New York was renowned for its pernicious dating scene. Nobody had any intention of wanting to commit. People dated numerous others at once on a never-ending loop, had casual sex at a rate I had never before seen. Which was fine – except nobody seemed fine. It seemed instead to sting people, dispirit them, cut their self-esteem. There was a joke that relationships started in November when it was too cold to go out, then ended in April when it was warm enough to meet someone new. Men catcalled you in the street with unceasing momentum. They followed you home. They reached out to touch you as you got off a bus. They interrupted your nights out with friends to talk about themselves and press you for a number. When it was too hot to sleep, I'd pull shorts on and a T-shirt, then sit with a book in an air-conditioned dive bar as men remarked if I really hadn't wanted to be picked up, I wouldn't be alone with my legs out. It was a chaotic place, of frenzied frat-boys on heat, and their 1920s outlook on clothes and skin. It was a sexually aggressive place, and it was fucking exhausting.

He told me he was monogamous; he didn't sleep around and hadn't been with anyone for a long time. It was up to me to decide if I wanted him – he wasn't possessive and wouldn't push.

But he made his presence known. He commented on my Instagram posts, left hearts under my pictures, put the palm of his hand on the back of mine, asked to kiss me, scratched the mosquito bite on the top of my knee, told me he hadn't felt like this for years. And asked for nothing else.

But this was also key: the behaviour without the 'contract'. The illusion of being the girlfriend, without the explicit words. The men who move to you with intimacy and closeness, who benefit from acting out the relationship, then later withhold respect, overrule your needs with 'I never actually said you were my girlfriend', 'We weren't even properly together', 'I didn't say it would be anything serious'.

I didn't realise then how heavily men relied on labels to consider a woman's humanity: girlfriend, wife, mother, daughter. The men who invest in feminism because they are the 'fathers of daughters', 'sons of mothers', 'husbands of wives', who need a woman to exist in proximity to them before we matter; the men who believe loyalty is reserved only for a girl-friend; the men who can only be held accountable by a wife. Women were not owed thoughtfulness, consistency and, above all else, kindness, if we hadn't proven our necessity first. The reward, it seemed, for demonstrating our value was to be classified suitably by some man.

I didn't have a conversation with *him* about what precisely our relationship was. He had said he was monogamous, expressed love and openly pursued me. For me it seemed clear. For him avoiding the explicit branding was how he would later negotiate his blame-lessness within a society that had already permitted him to do so.

But the foundation of our fantasy version was now there.

I went on holiday for some weeks. That was when he began to text the links: Wiki posts on how to date a person with autism, essays on how to be with someone who was agoraphobic, forums on what you can or cannot say to a person with complicated disabilities, YouTube videos, articles, short stories, Twitter threads, TV shows, podcasts, long text messages. It was shifting. And these were now the instructions for how to exist around a man just like him.

★

Women are taught to fear failure. To many of us failure simply means not having tried enough. Girls are taught to make it work, to not give up, to stick at things, fake it until you make it, keep going until it's fixed – the bare bones of being maternal: and to be maternal, in its most rightful sense, means abandoning nothing and no one.

The older you get as a woman, the more unpromising starting again can feel: I have known him since I was seventeen, who am I without him?; I am twenty-four, how can I financially afford to live in a new home alone?; I am thirty-five, will I make new friends when we share each other's?; I am forty-one, can I meet someone new in time to finally have kids with?; I am fifty-six, will I know how to pay for bills in my own name?; I am sixty-eight, I have never turned off the lights in an empty house and slept alone.

We keep going, so we don't bring shame to our families for divorcing, so we don't become gossip among our friends, so we don't elicit pity in the staff canteen, so we don't waste the cost of the wedding, so our kids don't come from a broken home, so he doesn't slap us, so the neighbours don't think he cheated, so he doesn't kill us, so we don't blame ourselves.

A few months into our relationship *he* went away. Australia, and Finland, and England, he said, for work. I was fed up.

His communication had lessened, his tone frequently disapproving, his obsession with how well I could manage his disabilities, as he called them, now persistent.

There wasn't an obvious moment when he, or the relationship, changed. Instances injected into the good, until the memory of the good was the only thing left and keeping you. Where now the goal of the relationship was a journey to finding a way back to the person you loved; more importantly, back to the person who first loved you.

New York was tense as Trump's election grew closer. I watched the debates in Williamsburg bars, twinkling car lights on the bridge above, chins turned and twisted up to screens, the overdone bar small talk replaced by optimistic chatter for Hillary's win. I simply couldn't understand it. Couldn't understand the cheery hope when the unavoidable was gawking at us. In a friend's brownstone in Crown Heights we drank beers and threw cigarette butts out the window on election night. We were a room full of brown people from brown backgrounds. When Trump won, the only two white people cried. They held each other and sobbed, and someone said, *Why you crying, you should have known*, and no one hugged goodbye, and someone slammed their beer back and opened another, and someone else ordered cabs for all the brown people who lived walking distance; because not a single thing, or person, felt safe anymore. I wanted to leave that party, leave the city, leave Trump's brand-new America that wasn't new at all, leave *him*, and his podcasts and his audio-books and his research on why I could never get it right.

And then the text message arrived. *He* had tried to kill himself, somewhere in Melbourne, between jobs, and he was in a suicide prevention clinic, and needed only my support and care.

I felt held in position, breathless.

The next time I'd feel the same would be a few months later. On a night when it snowed, and his phone rang to voicemail, and the white outside suffocated me, snared me in a space, that snow, that fucking snow that kept me in place. And in the morning his message came, that his mother was dead, gone, and I lay in bed, face down on my pregnant belly, as though choking on mouthfuls of snow, that fucking snow, shovelled into my throat.

ii.

In the marketplace they are piling the dry
    sticks.
A thicket of shadows is a poor coat. I
    inhabit
The wax image of myself, a doll's body.
Sickness begins here: I am the dartboard
    for witches.
Only the devil can eat the devil out.
In the month of red leaves I climb to a
    bed of fire.

— Sylvia Plath, 'Witch Burning'

Two weeks after the clinic I flew to Vancouver to perform at a literary festival. When I look back, I know I was only able to get there with the determined guidance of those who described to me what days should look like: brush your teeth, put on deodorant, open a bag, put clothes inside, make a cup of tea, find your shoes, put them on, get on the subway, text us from the subway, this is your connecting train to the airport, take this too, text us when you are on that as well.

In Canada old friends greeted and gathered me. We were doing the show together and between rehearsals and sound-checks they reminded me, with a kind of ferocity only old friends possess, of the person I had been in London before all this. I did the show, I think on a kind of autopilot that I remembered from starting out, doing poetry in back rooms of east London pubs. I had, briefly, remembered what it was to be alive.

On my return, arriving at Newark airport, I searched his name. What I found was a recording of a comedy show he had done in Manhattan four nights before the clinic. The date of the show aligned with the night he had told me he was in Atlanta. The night, he had said, his mother died.

In the recording he can be heard introducing himself to the audience. He is cold and disparaging, and continues his set with a sequence of statements I will not call jokes. He tells a story about having sex with a woman in her sleep. He tells another about inserting the morning-after pill, known as Plan B, inside women's vaginas. He tells the crowd he has intentions to conceal Plan B inside women's food and drinks.

'Are there any Muslims here?' he asks. 'None? Good. I've never met a good or kind one. I'd be happy if they all died.'

On an icy Jersey train platform, I broke down. I thought back to the night this set had been recorded: the snowstorm, and how I had sat alone in my apartment watching the empty white street from my window, the thickness of the snow, how heavy it was. And I was trapped by it, terrified, registering every cramp in my body, had pushed my palm against my stomach as though it would tell me what to do, as though, for a moment, I was not totally fucking alone.

Elsewhere, he recounted fantasies of violent coerced abortions and the mass genocide of Muslims. The snowstorm did not stop him. Nothing did. Finally, I thought, he would be happy – his pregnant Muslim girlfriend was at home, and he had killed me on stage.

*

Even then, I kept searching his name. I was still looking for answers back then. Looking to make sense of the days and weeks before the clinic. Was he having a mental breakdown triggered by the grief of the abortion? Had he met someone else and left me for her? I needed something tangible, either to vindicate myself with, or punish myself further. I had believed his final words – that no one should love me – I regarded them as truth. Had I not been ruined or unworthy of love before this, I thought, his actions had since made sure I now was. And so I needed to know precisely what had made me unlovable. Not so I might improve myself once I had an extensive catalogue of all that was wrong, but so I could confirm that I was right to feel I had never been good enough.

My searches became obsessive. I scoured his social media, googled every variation of his name I could think of. I went back years. I analysed the emotion on his face in photographs, studied the captions and hashtags he wrote beneath for hidden meaning and secret messages. Was he trying to communicate with me through his posts? I wondered. I examined his posture in pictures with women – how close were they standing, was a leg or a hand or a head tilt an indication of flirtation, coquettish and romantic? I went through his new followers on Instagram. Then studied the profiles of those who were women. I dissected their pages as meticulously. Manically.

I considered these women through his eyes.

Was this someone he would find attractive? Was her body better than mine? Her bottom in a thong bikini on a trip to Cancún, a crop top and low-rise jeans at a family barbecue, her thighs in a dress as she took in the view from a balcony. Was she prettier? Short hair suited her in a photograph two years back, a sun-kissed selfie in minimal make-up, her nose looked good from every angle. What was her personality? High energy, a video of her dancing at a girls' night out, her tongue sticking out in a photo, champagne flute raised above her head, dispersed quotes about meditation and living well and working out.

I sent screenshots to my girlfriends, demanding to know if these women were any good. Their smiles, the life still within them to be sexy and fun and happy, the joy – everything he had consumed, that was no longer left in me. I couldn't compete with them. The holidays they enjoyed, the jobs they worked, the clothes they wore, that their bodies, bigger and smaller, looked better – it was all better, they were better. And yet . . .

She took a lot of selfies for someone who claimed to be a feminist in one of her posts, don't you think? She captioned a picture of her cleavage once with the unrelated philosophies of Rumi because she's clearly quite stupid. Remember that group photo from Christmas I sent you? She didn't look as good in that one. Now that you mention it, her body looked a little different in one of her at a wedding. In fact, at her brother's graduation her nose was a little big. She was up herself, had nothing to say for herself, no ambition, no aspiration, just wanted to look good in photos, just wanted a boyfriend, probably your boyfriend, she was desperate, too conventionally pretty actually, probably a slag, too sexy, and too opinionated, and too available, and took far too many holidays, and too hyper, and too confident, and too needy, and . . .

When you consider women through the eyes of men, you will view them only as men do. You will pit yourself against every woman. And not one of you will be good enough.

These women were not a hazard. They were just out there getting on with their lives. Some of them had even worked out how to like themselves, thankfully, and the others were just trying.

They deserved to be sexy and beautiful and full of joy, in their social media, and in real life.

He was the threat. Not other women. And soon, that would become even clearer.

★

The streets of Bed-Stuy became a place that learned to accommodate the nature of my moods as quickly as I grew to navigate them: the three old men stretched over wooden chairs in front of the boarded-up mechanic's; the Yemeni dudes who'd sell you cheap counterfeit cigarettes once they knew you were local. The dive bar with the owner's truck parked outside, and the locals who took their dogs to sit on stools beside them as they shouted answers at *Jeopardy!* playing on the small screen above their heads. We were learning to move collectively, and the importance of community would soon prove to be of absolute necessity.

A month after the clinic, in a bar at the end of my road, I typed his name into Instagram. I was still terrorising myself. Still hoping to find evidence that he was better off without me.

Instead, what I saw was a black and white drawing of his face in profile. It had been posted in November 2016. The day of the clinic had been two months later, in January 2017. By this time, it was February and New York was no warmer. The picture was well drawn, the lines thin and shaded well, the face indisputably his. It was accompanied with a hashtag of his full name, which is how I had come to find it. And this comment: 'Unfortunately the guy in the picture turned out to be a psychopath.'

I ordered another drink. In the last month drinking was mostly all I knew to do. I started early and finished when the bars closed. When I knew I could pass out in the dullness and stillness of five in the morning, when I was too tired to cry.

The image hung in the air. It had been posted by a woman called Zoe. A woman who, from what I could gather from her social media, lived in Australia and shared cheery photographs of herself with friends in sunny outdoor spaces. Amidst them, this stark image of him.

She had posted it during the weeks he had told me he was recovering from his suicide attempt at a clinic in Melbourne. I had been beside myself those weeks. Frantic, I remembered. I had worn his depression back then, carried it as a way to keep him less alone over there.

A tiredness grew over me. I ordered another drink. Then another. I sat with my head in my hands, clichéd in my reaction. I must have written and rewritten my message to Zoe at least a dozen times. I believed she would think I was crazy. I believed I was crazy. Unlovable and damaged, as he had said.

And then, she replied. With a kind of goodwill that comes from someone who had expected I would reach out — if not *me*, then *somebody*.

From a bar in Bed-Stuy and a home across the world in Melbourne, two women who hadn't known of the other wrote back and forth. Zoe told me her story. They had met on Tinder, she said. They had dated for the month — October 2016 — that he had been in Australia for work.

What had happened between them? I asked. 'There was an obvious barrier between us,' she wrote in her message to me. 'He would be extremely giving via text, but face to face there was something lacking completely. He would be pretty erratic at times. He was cold and mean — not to me, but in all the stories he told. He made himself out to be an asshole, but when I pulled him up on this he would tell me stories to paint himself in a completely different light. For example, he told me that he took his own friend to the police station after the friend admitted to date-raping a girl. He took a very feminist approach when telling me this. But the timing of the story, and his obvious intention to copy my ideals straight after I told him he was a bit of an asshole, seemed off. He also retold stories, but the details wouldn't match.'

I knew this about him. That a flicker of disapproval could trigger a reversal in his narrative. Then, he would talk incessantly, twisting his thoughts in different directions until you had forgotten the root of his sentences, or felt too fatigued to follow up.

She went on. 'He would message me really amazing things but then go off radar. I told him I felt like he was playing a game. He said he wasn't playing and that he loved me – by then, I had met him twice.'

At the end of October he returned to New York. Zoe had already posted the drawing she had done of him, initially a kind of private joke between the two of them, his name hash-tagged beneath with no real purpose. She reflected on their month together, then wrote the comment about him being a psychopath as a throwaway remark to a friend. There had been no mention or sign of an attempted suicide, nor a clinic, she said.

'You're actually the second person to reach out to me,' she wrote. 'The first was a woman called Jessica.' The message went on: 'She lives in New York.'

★

I know now what I did not know then: that absolution comes in many forms; where I could not acquit him, I would begin to forgive myself.

I was sitting in a darkened bar on Myrtle, illuminated only by the red and blue lights of firetrucks and police cars outside, when a reply from Jessica arrived. It was frank. It was straight to the point and, much like Zoe's response, seemed prepared and somehow expecting: 'I'm sorry to hear that you also had quite the ordeal with him,' Jessica began. 'I funded his entire "work" trip this past fall. I also got pregnant by him.'

A society, by necessity, relies on patterned and consistent behaviour, and soon I would understand the full darkness of this. My body still believed it was pregnant. It still ached a certain way, still bled, and a violence now made its way through me. I remember wanting to break walls with my hands. To set streets aflame and walk into the burning rage of it.

Jessica agreed to meet the following night. I asked where she lived. Bed-Stuy, she replied. Only a few blocks away.

She was already sat at the bar on Tompkins Avenue, halfway between our apartments, when I got there. The kind of place that bustles with winding bodies at the weekend but remains uninhabited midweek, a few barstools in the darkness of the space. We ordered wine, filled our glasses with ice to dilute the sweetened taste of house white, both nervous yet composed, gathered.

'Did you know about me?' she asked. I told her the truth – No. I hadn't even suspected a woman before the clinic, or two.

Jessica was gentle, while not a gentle woman. That is to say she was steely, smart and bright-eyed. She told me she had met him in spring 2016, not long before I had. They had met on Tinder, as we had. She described their first date. It was at a comedy night he was performing at, somewhere he had also taken me to. She named his friends who had joined them, men we had both met briefly to begin with, before dates trailed off into nights at home. She had never been to his apartment. His roommates did not want visitors, he told her. Then, for a period, the apartment was riddled with bedbugs and no one was allowed there, not even him.

I had also never been to his apartment. His sister was in town for the summer, he had said, and was living in his bedroom while he slept on the sofa. At the end of summer things had changed again for him, and he had lost his place, he told me, and was crashing with friends.

For a long while he kept his things at hers: clothes, toiletries, his protein shakes, a laptop. She was describing my relationship, from their dates to the very last item in her house. I listened to her as though I were talking.

She became pregnant in August 2016. I became pregnant a few months later. They broke up in December of that same year. He was gone from my life a few weeks after that.

I was with him when she was pregnant. She was with him when I was pregnant. Each point landed as a strike. This gathering of revelations was a weight.

The closer we came to making sense of it, the more senseless it became.

I did not need to imagine the circumstances under which she became pregnant. By now, I asked questions knowing the answers: Had he told you he was autistic? That he had lost the love of his life in an accident? Did he tell you he had never been with a woman without using condoms before, and it was important you became his 'first'? Quick-fire round: every answer was a yes. And the clinic? I asked. 'Queens. He took me to the one in Queens.'

I remembered the way I had howled outside the building. I remembered losing my balance, both in that moment and the weeks that followed.

'I'm thirty-six. It's not like I don't want to be a mother one day – I do,' Jessica said, 'but he was really unsupportive and I don't know if I was expecting that. The next day, after he found out I was pregnant, I went to work and he sent me these long texts about how, of course, he wanted to have children with me. And of course we're going to be together forever, but we couldn't have kids right now because he was travelling too much with work. He's not ready, and he wants to be able to support a family. I didn't even really feel like I made the decision to have an abortion.'

As she talked, I thought of my own choices that were not really choices.

Did you just feel exhausted? I asked. 'I was so fucking exhausted. I didn't want to have an abortion, but I didn't want to be in this situation anymore. I even said to him, if he didn't want to come with me to the clinic it would be totally fine. But he reassured me he would be there and that we were in it together. Then, the night before my appointment, he wasn't showing up. It was two in the morning and I didn't know where he was. He finally came at four in the morning. When we woke up he was trying to get out of going to the clinic. I think he was always going to come with me, just to make sure I went through with it, but he needed to stress me out more first, torture me.'

On the morning of my abortion, he had also been late. The night before he had been in Atlanta, he had said, signing his mother's death certificate. He had taken a red-eye flight back to be with me but the trains from JFK, he said, were delayed and so he would be cutting it close. I remembered checking the service on the subway that morning. Everything seemed to be running fine.

'In the car on the way to the clinic he kept talking.' Jessica laughed a little, as though I knew what she meant. I did. 'Talking and talking. It was exhausting. He kept fucking talking. He just wouldn't let it be about me for one morning.' She paused. By then we were both thinking about the clinic and him within it. 'They took my blood and left me there for a minute. At one point I got up and peered out into the waiting room to see if he was there. He was. When they asked if I wanted him to come into the room with me I said no, because, honestly, I had this weird moment

where I just thought he's not going to be out there –
like he could have left. I remember feeling very alone.
Even though he was out there, it felt like he wasn't.
Then, when I came out, he didn't skip a beat. He
went back to talking about whatever fucking thing
he'd been talking about before.'

What I had needed back then was for Jessica to tell
me what those following hours had looked like.

I was desperate to know who he might have been
when a woman walks from the doctor's office to the
waiting room and her partner is still there.

I had imagined it before. Many times, in fact. As
though on another day he might have been a man
who grieved the decision with me.

'We got home,' Jessica said, 'and there was the
prescription to collect – anti-nausea, and pain-relief
meds. He said he had a headache so I needed to get
them myself. I remember going to the pharmacy in
the heat. And he wanted me to get him blue Gatorade
and chocolate milk. I kept thinking he'd be gone by
the time I got back. He wasn't. But later, he went into
the bathroom for a long while, and when he came
back out he said his dad was in town from Atlanta
and he needed to go meet him.' She was laughing
less lightly now. 'I thought, "*What?* Your dad, who
you hate, is suddenly in New York to see you?"' I
understood this – the things we recognise as ridiculous
yet we suspend our disbelief.

'He said he was going to take his dad for a drink locally, then bring him back so I could meet him,' Jessica continued. 'I thought it was odd, but at least it was better than him disappearing and not coming back at all. Which, of course, he actually did. At some point in the evening I messaged to ask if he was really coming back. He said because I was questioning and doubting him I had made him not want to come back at all. I was agitating his autism. He said I had forced him to now stay away.'

And the next day – I asked – the day it passed from your body?

'Still no sign of him. He was messaging me hateful shit. Not once did he ask how I was doing. And then I went to take the pain-relief medication during the home stage of the abortion, and they were gone. He had taken them all.'

I realised then that to be loathsome cannot be contained. Nor does it go by any other name. His hatred was his own Groundhog Day.

Jessica texted him and asked if he had really taken the medication to ease her abortion, and why. His only reply was to laugh.

★

There was no version of him during those hours with Jessica that was better. No alternative world where had I perhaps asked him to come into the clinician's room with me, or hidden my spare key, or argued less in those months before, or argued more, or laughed, or danced, or bent a different way, or been a different woman, he would have been there for me in those hours. There was no outcome – no matter who I could have been – where his necessity was not simply to hurt.

'I don't know why I stayed with him,' Jessica said. But she did. She was worn out. As I had been. Confidence fractured, unable to trust our own judgement after months of being told we simply would not get it right. In this instance failing all his mental health demands had swallowed us whole.

There was always something ready to swallow you. Not just with this man, but others too. How often have we been told the house wasn't clean enough. Your look on a night out was never the right one. The meals you cooked were at the wrong time, the wrong portion, the wrong taste.

Your shortcomings were absolute, and terminal. You weren't running behind at the supermarket because there was plenty to stock up on, it was because you were *always* late. You didn't have a difference of opinion on which video games were the most fun to play, you simply *always* had bad taste. You didn't drop that pesto jar as it slipped from your hands, you were *always* careless. You didn't sleep through your alarm because you had insomnia until the early hours, you were *always* lazy. You didn't say that thing to his colleagues about getting drunk in your student years because it was an entertaining story, you were *always* inappropriate. You didn't dance for hours at his cousin's wedding because it was fun, you were *always* embarrassing yourself.

Always wrong. Always overreacting. Always looking for something to moan about. You always act like that. You always think that. You would say that, wouldn't you – you always do.

After a while, you become 'always'. The total sum of not enough – always.

Who else would want a woman defined by her deficiencies? Then, are we not in gratitude as women, obligated to the man who stands by, at what is now his own expense? And so, at the staff Christmas party your husband flirts in front of you with a woman you've had your suspicions about, and you stay. The father of your kids teaches them a nickname he's given you taking the piss out of your weight, and you stay. Your boyfriend spends three hundred quid with the lads at the weekend then yells at you when there's not enough money for bills, and you stay. Your partner doesn't pick up the phone when you're depressed and need help because it's too heavy, too boring, too much, he had other shit on, and you stay. Or he doesn't touch you anymore but won't tell you why, and you stay. Or he blocks your number after every small fight until you learn to stop asking for what you need, and you stay. He dashes food you made across the room because you were too chatty with the man two doors down, and you stay. Or he chokes you in the middle of the street because you were crying too hard, and you stay.

★

Or, in this case, he steals your pain-relief medication after an abortion, and you stay.

This is 'always'. Locked into a place.

If I had been in a better place in my life, I would not have accepted *his* declarations of loving me so early on. I might have recognised it for what it was, a snare. Had I not just come out of a burdensome long-term relationship, alone in a city across the world from what I knew, with only a few friends and an all-consuming loneliness, I would not have needed feverish endorsement from a person I did not know.

It wasn't love that kept me in place, it was the concept of it. The legend of love as conquering all. It would take all my afflictions away, replace my self-loathing with self-assurance, or so I believed. If he loved me it might mean there was, after all, something to love about me. I bent myself to his every need to keep what being loved by a man had come to mean for me – that I wasn't entirely worthless, not entirely a piece of shit. The concept of being loved, and the fast-track route to healing that I thought it provided, became more important than how that love made me feel, which was often anxious and dreadful. Keeping him happy, keeping him healthy, meant keeping his love, even if I was no longer either of those things myself.

After all, hadn't I, before my third meeting with him, searched online 'Am I dating a psychopath?' The signs were there. The immediate full-on declarations, the stories that already didn't quite add up. And had I been less vulnerable, less unguarded, less anguished, less isolated, I might have valued my apprehensions over hope. Hopefulness, and the concept of love, became so commanding I ignored what I had already picked up on about him, and others, so early on in our relationship. I endured the ridicule, the silent treatment, being goaded, undermined, persuading myself they had not been texting or meeting other women. I accepted every lie, made my own excuses for why the bank statement showed they had been to a different bar from the one they had claimed to be in, why they began to take their phone to the bathroom when they hadn't done before, why they didn't reply to my messages, or show up when they said they would. I did the work for them, created half of the fabrications on their behalf, so I wouldn't be a failure, so I wouldn't have to start again, so I wouldn't lose value by losing the concept and hope of love.

The only thing I seemed to agree on with men like this was that I was the problem. And their bad behaviour could therefore be traced back to my short-comings. If I couldn't be trusted to get anything right, how could I trust my own gut? And so I listened to him over myself. Over and over again, until we were all in too deep.

★

We had been taught long before *him* that our purpose as women was directly related to our ability to care for men, and to their standards. In a bar on Tompkins, Jessica went on: 'I was so worried about him all the time. I thought maybe he was hurting, and had issues with his dad being in town. I thought maybe he needs those meds more than me. But everything was about him. I honestly think the only reason he didn't leave me at the clinic too is because I was paying for him by then. It was a few weeks before his trip to Europe, Japan, Australia, and he needed me for that trip – I had already agreed to pay.'

By that time he had left his day job over, he claimed, serious allegations he had made against the company. It was going to be a sure win for him, he said, but in the meantime he needed to borrow money from her to stay afloat. In September 2016 he would be working on film sets in various locations across the world. The salary was good, he told her, and he would be able to pay her back. But here was the catch: his bosses on the film set couldn't front the money for his flights and accommodation. Jessica would have to pay for him to be there, do the work, and only then could he pay her back for it all.

Soon after, he began to reveal more and more ailments and illnesses: his depression had worsened, he had agoraphobia and could no longer travel on the subway, he wasn't eating, and was falling apart under the pressure of his own mental health. He needed to be on Jessica's Uber account so he could travel to her more easily, and to his comedy shows. (I realise now who had actually paid for my Uber home the first night I had met him.) She put him on all her accounts for groceries and restaurant deliveries too.

Shortly after her abortion, he left for two months on the work trip. While he was away Jessica began to receive messages from his mother. His mother, he had told her, had cancer. In her messages she told Jessica how grateful she felt knowing that her son was with someone who made him happy. It was her dying wish they make it work. Jessica and his mother began to message often, and it was his mother who told Jessica he was having breakdowns overseas and needed more money for suicide prevention clinics and medication too. By the end of 2016, Jessica had given him $30,000.

Jessica had grown agitated. She suspected other women, which was something I had not. I had viewed him as someone so engrossed with his all-consuming mental health issues I didn't see how he had the energy for anything else. Jessica, on the other hand, had begun to confront him. He responded with screenshots of various Instagram accounts. These were some of his closest friends, he said, and these were the people who were likely to keep popping up on his feed – people she need not worry about. Jessica took out her phone and scrolled the images he had sent her: the boyfriend of a woman he had mentioned to us both, other comedians, a few women neither of us recognised, a few we did, and me. I swore loudly. He had sent it to her near the time of her abortion – my face, my name, now an alibi. Did you suspect I was with him? I asked. 'Actually, no. I guess you weren't so new in his life back then, so I hadn't picked up on your presence on his social media in the same way. I was mostly worried about him meeting new girls while he was away. I thought the picture of you was a random, and I thought nothing of it.'

When he returned to New York after two months abroad, Jessica and I were both by now weary. We had simultaneously endured an arduous long-distance relationship with a man who had, according to him, a significant downward spiral with his health and been committed to several overseas clinics. I was tired and fed up, if not with him, certainly with the perpetual worry.

Neither of us had mastered how (if such a thing were possible) to faultlessly be with a man who had his kind of depression, a man who claimed to be autistic, a man with endless specific requirements for how you must treat him without being ignorant towards his disabilities. He reminded us of this most days. We were always failing. I thought back to all the nights

44

we had planned to see each other, how he would say he was in a cab on the way, or nearby, then not show up at all. Eventually, I would hear from him. He had been sick, he had gone to hospital, his agoraphobia had got the better of him. There was little apology if any at all. We were always to blame for expecting any better from him. Always to apologise for how difficult it had been for him.

Yet there was very little of his autism and agoraphobia that resembled what I knew of these conditions, or the people I knew who had them. But I am not a specialist, and to challenge or disbelieve would be cruel on my part. I read the articles he sent. I read articles he had not. I asked for nothing and expected less. I cried alone, frustrated, never showing him for fear of harming him.

I had seen other women do this. Watched them peel every layer of themselves until there was nothing left but the idea of women as carers, givers and maternal. He had wanted the unconditional love of a mother, yet without allowing us the right to be.

Where we responded differently was that Jessica had snapped. Perhaps because she had given him so much money to look after himself with. She went through his emails, his messages, everything on his computer, which he had left open in her apartment. 'There was a suitcase full of things that belonged to a well-known singer he knew,' Jessica said, 'her jewellery, letters, napkins with her lipstick on, photo-booth pictures of them together. It was a shrine to her. There were also messages between him and other women. But the craziest thing was a saved piece of text in his notes, which was a message I had received word for word from his mother. He was pasting those messages and sending them to me as though they were from her.'

Jessica ended it with him. 'He just had this soulless look in his eyes. The next day, when I was at work, he took all his things and charged me for a two-hundred-dollar Uber.' Things had gone missing from her apartment too – a pull-up exercise bar and some alcohol that had, as it turned out, made its way to my apartment. She cancelled all her cards and changed the locks. In mid-January 2017, a month after their break-up – and a day after I had been to the clinic – she came home and saw he had left his spare key, now redundant, in her door.

★

I asked Jessica how she had found Zoe. 'I was looking for answers. I felt crazy. You messaged her only a few weeks later.' Jessica had also gone looking on Twitter. There she found another woman, Alyse, who had been his girlfriend in 2011. 'She had a Twitter post that read, "I still have my ex's current girlfriends reach out to me, and all I can say is run." I messaged her too, and she told me he had put her through the works.

46

They lived together for three years. He worked in Los Angeles for a while, and was accused of having stolen tens of thousands from them. She picked him up from the police station the next morning. She said she'd lost most of her hair by the end of it all. He's been like this for a long time.'

★

In the months that followed, Jessica and I stayed in touch. I was learning to breathe on my own again, and she had put her sleuthing behind her. Over time I began to laugh again, to dance, slowly. Like this, I was learning to control my body once more. I remembered how to write, something I had lost for half a year. On the anniversary of the would-be birth, friends came to my apartment and we celebrated. I had wanted to think of that day not as a loss, but as a marker that I was still alive. I had wanted to thank the people who had been my hands and legs and brain as I had been teaching myself to be again.

Jessica and I continued to meet for drinks. Over time our conversations moved from him to us – our lives, our work, and films, and politics – to who we are. The snow had melted and Brooklyn was again a place of street parties and Cîroc, loud car stereos and frustrating subway journeys to the Rockaways. One night I unwittingly found myself on Jessica's date with a new man. Another time she had, somehow, ended up on one of

47

mine. We joked – perhaps neither of us would date again without first vetting each other's choices.

Weekends at Coney Island became fewer as the weather shifted. Carved pumpkins formed rows on the steps of neighbours' brownstones. I texted Jessica. It was by now November 2017 and, if calculations were to be believed as wholly accurate, a year to the day since I had become pregnant. I wanted to plan a drink, catch-up, gossip. Perhaps I reached out to her knowing the date, knowing it meant nothing and everything at once. I remember clearly where I was, sat in a bar in Fort Greene on the corner of Vanderbilt, a glass of wine after a meeting, green and white tiles on the walls. And as we texted back and forth Jessica checked the Instagram post, almost intuitively. 'Holy shit.' One of her replies read. 'Have you seen Zoe's illustration lately?'

It had been nearly a year since Jessica and I had found each other. In that time, it appeared, more women had reached out to Zoe. She had edited the caption under her post to read: 'Comments on this illustration continuously get taken down. They say things about the person being a psychopath and dangerous to women. I leave it here because it is true. It is not meant to shame, but to alert women that they may be in danger when becoming close to this man.'

Beneath it, a woman called Samantha commented: 'I got out of a relationship with him not too long ago. Everything you say is true. Told me his mom was dying of cancer and stole close to nine thousand dollars from me.'

Under that, a reply from someone called Kay: 'Same thing happened to me. I dated him this past summer. The mom with cancer lie. The taking money and not paying it back. He also had a girlfriend the entire time we were together.'

Then, Olivia: 'So sorry he did this to you too. Took five thousand dollars from me. Lived with me for a year while he impregnated and stole from other women. He's a piece of garbage, and I bet you're wonderful. Be kind to yourself as you work through this.'

I think back to a night in north London: the women of a friendship group gathered around a kitchen table, red wine stains on our teeth and lips. We recounted stories, shared moments of the degrading shit our exes and dates and colleagues and strangers had done to us. We shook our heads, rolled our eyes, interjected with, *Oh God, that reminds me of . . . Did I tell you about the other . . .? . . . That's so much like the time . . .*

. . . The woman who had been followed from the bus, who asked a group of men nearby for help. 'What makes you think I won't be the one to rape you?' one of them said. There was the woman whose pub manager scheduled shifts so she always worked late and alone with him. And the woman whose boyfriend took photos of her secretly as she bent over to pull up her tights. And the woman whose ex told her to go straight to the gym to get her figure back after she'd given birth. And the woman whose husband shagged someone at a party when she was at home recovering from an operation. And the woman whose ex posted a Facebook photo of a new girlfriend not even six weeks after her miscarriage. And the woman whose friend pushed his erection against her after they had passed out in the same bed. There was the woman who had thrown up at a party and passed out, whose friend had put his fingers inside her. And the woman who kept asking a date to put the condom back on until she eventually kicked him out. And the woman whose boyfriend insisted he go through her phone daily. And the woman whose ex texted her endlessly throughout the day, professing either love or hatred in every fevered message.

Women have always told these stories to each other, within the safety of each other. This was nothing new. And I felt this again — that the bodies of women were a *chain*, bound by history. And if people were going to keep insisting that our bodies were not really *ours*, we would stand side by side to show where one ended and the other began.

*

That night, I sat alone in a bar in Fort Greene on the corner of Vanderbilt, and Jessica and I texted wildly. We hastily pulled together a list of *his* friends we had met in those early days, or he had mentioned repeatedly, comedians, ex-colleagues, the people he seemed to interact with the most. We tagged them. *Look at who your boy is!* we wrote. *See for yourselves!* And we went to bed feeling giddy.

By the following morning, his friends had commented. Some were horrified. Some publicly expressed that they were. There is a difference.

Those friends told other friends. Those comedians told other comedians. In only a few hours even more people had come to look at it. Hundreds of comments beneath Zoe's post.

The women he had hurt arrived in vast quantities. They shared their own stories. Women from all over the world: London, Oslo, Helsinki, Sydney. The places Jessica had funded trips to. Some places she hadn't.

I am sorry – we wrote to each other. I am sorry. I remembered the clinic. I am sorry.

And the voices came.

iii.

Paradox girl, mighty woman,
you are the thing that terrifies them.

Both monster and maiden, both cure and
    poison,
all of these things, and at the same time
    human.

Defined by no man, you are your own
    story,
blazing through the world, turning
    history into herstory.

And when they dare to tell you about
all the things you cannot be,
you smile and tell them,
'I am both war and woman and you
    cannot stop me.'

— *Nikita Gill, 'An Ode To Fearless Women'*

Freezer spells are designed to do just that – freeze out something, or someone, from your life. These kinds of spells might be done with herbs; red pepper to make someone's lies burn in their mouth, poppy seeds to confuse a person, or alum to silence someone's speech.

Sometimes the spell used a cow's tongue, sliced straight through the middle, with a person's name written on a piece of paper inserted in the slit to shut them up.

In Helsinki a woman opened her freezer and found a note that had been left inside. On it, a list of names. One name was mine. Beneath, in capitals and boldly underlined, *he* had written: 'All my enemies fall!'

★

I don't know how he first came to see the Instagram post. What I do know is that he did everything in his power to bury it. It seemed that he had been aware of it as early as the start of 2017, around the same time Jessica and myself had seen it, and months before the post escalated fully later that year.

'At some point he realised,' Zoe said, 'but I had at least three women reach out in those first few months and you all had pretty traumatic stories. I knew it was important people could find the post. So I kept his name hash-tagged under it knowing there was nothing he could do about that, knowing also that his name is uncommon and he strives for social media presence.' Zoe had also hash-tagged words like 'dangerous' and 'be careful' beneath the post, and read the Instagram community guidelines to make sure she wasn't breaking any.

As 2017 went on, more and more women privately got in touch with her. Many had their own traumatic stories about him. Others got in touch with Zoe to say he had asked them to report Zoe's account. Within a year of the post being up, she had received around twenty direct messages. 'I felt an overwhelming sense of responsibility to support each of the women who contacted me, but I also felt like the thing I should do is connect them with each other. It was a strange position to be in. He didn't manage to hurt me, but I was seemingly in the middle of it all.'

I doubt it's a coincidence that *his* post detonated in November 2017, only a month after the MeToo movement really blew up and Harvey Weinstein's victims were finally given a voice. I don't think any of us had imagined the Instagram post about *him* would take off quite as it did, but the *chain* was now forming in front of us, both personally and globally.

The comments told a repeated and all too familiar story, spanning many years and with countless women. One wrote: 'I am one of the women as well. He took money from me. Hundreds of euros and fooled me to buy flights to meet him in New York. He also lied. Cheated. Scammed.'

Another: 'Thank God he never took money, but he deleted all my files from my computer and smashed my memory card. Took over my Facebook and left a "spell" in my freezer. He stole money from at least one other woman too in Helsinki and she took it to the police but they weren't able to do anything about it.'

★

In November 2017, as hundreds of comments stretched beneath the post, it was clear he had a template, which he applied every time. We learned from each other that he told us he was in hospital or a suicide clinic, asked us for money to pay for his meds or the admission fee, or one treatment or another that would save his life. Every woman, however, had been told a different (nameless) suicide prevention clinic, including one in Canada, England, Russia and, as he had told me, Australia.

In fact, his mental health had been quite the feature throughout his relationships with the women he dated. 'He always played the depression, autism or agoraphobia card when things didn't add up,' another woman wrote, 'he tried to make me feel bad or seem insensitive for asking questions, pointing out that you wouldn't ask a blind man why he couldn't see.'

In another comment a young woman wrote that she had met him four years prior, in her early twenties, on another dating site. She had given him, the man she loved, all of her savings – $9,400 – to help with legal fees for a heroic incident in which he had been protecting a friend in a brawl but had unwittingly assaulted a police officer. He was, he told her, owed thousands elsewhere and would be going to Germany for a sound engineering job that would pay him well. The money, he said, would be returned to her quickly. Instead, he had taken the money and gone travelling around Asia and London with it, telling her that the money she gave him had been a gift, before later denying she had given him anything at all. She wrote on the Instagram thread: 'Thankfully, I no longer break down in my car, no longer rage into the air. This moment gives me hope and validation.'

All these relationships overlapped with other women, many, *many* women. Most wrote of giving him money, of losing items from their homes, pregnancies, lies, and his mother who was, as it turns out, coming back to life again and again, but unfortunately dying of cancer on the regular.

It is tiresome living in a world where experience only becomes truth in volume, truth validated only in numbers. But I understood that this is how it goes. And so did he.

Mania consumed him. A rage grew within. I had seen this the day of the clinic, once I had messaged his friend and aired *his* dirty laundry. Within a few days there were five hundred comments and then the post was deleted.

Unfortunately for him, one of the women he had abused worked for Instagram. By morning, the post (much like his mother) was fully resurrected.

Now with the post back up, he did a strange thing: he created two new accounts. He called one I Love___, with his first name, and the other I Love___, using his first and last names. It said it all. He loved himself. But, more sinisterly, he was making us proclaim our love for him each time we typed the profile's name to check for any update or response, which many of us were doing. There were two reasons we were looking: firstly, to keep ahead of his next move; but secondly, if I am completely honest, because it was a kind of glorious ghoulish car crash unfolding in front of our eyes. He was falling apart in real time and, frankly, it was wonderful to see.

Now, from these two accounts he posted long paragraphs, switching nonsensically between the two slightly varying names. He wrote that he had a fiancée whom he had met in early 2017 in London. He said he was a better man with her. She had given him the peace none of us could. He accused us of having an agenda fuelled by jealousy since he had moved on with her. He claimed his fiancée had seen the post – by then over forty women had described the tens of thousands he had taken from them individually, multiple pregnancies, and the lies involving his mother's health and fate – and she had laughed about it with her friends. He referred to himself as peaceful and godly. He claimed that if any of what we had said was true – that he had used people for affection, money, and a desire to be wined and dined – he had learned this from every woman that had ever existed.

'I understand your anger,' he wrote publicly to us, 'I did lie to you, saying I cared about you, liked you, thought you were attractive, pretended not to care about your gross bodies, your messed-up teeth, lying about loving your personalities that were as captivating as shoe inserts.'

He thanked us all for reminding him of the good man he knows himself to be.

Between both accounts he posted pictures of Buddha and Christ and screenshots of the same lengthy public post he had written, over and over again. He shared links to podcasts of him speaking to the woman who was now his fiancée. He talked and talked at great length of how his only crime had been to cheat, which he had done because he had never before loved a woman like he loved her. She remained mostly silent throughout the recordings. At times she could be heard yawning. He was by now frenzied.

Yet amidst his ongoing outbursts, the stories of betrayal, the heartbreak, the surreal mayhem of it all – there was a kind of jubilation, relief, an elation. We made fun of him openly in the comments. We mocked his absurdity. To the individual, what he had done was isolating and bleak, but to the *chain* locking itself around him, the man was a farce.

Had you heard the story about him being raised by his Japanese martial arts instructor?! The plot from *Karate Kid*! Had you heard the disturbing story about putting a woman's cat in the microwave?! The plot from *Bad Boy Bubby*! What about the aunt who worked as a lawyer when you threatened to sue him? The same aunt that worked for an abortion clinic when you were pregnant? The same one who worked in immigration, when he was threatening to have you deported from America? That same aunt who also worked for an airline company when he was flying back and forth to Atlanta eighteen times a week?

The instagram post was not a photograph of him. This mattered. It was a black and white illustration, a vision of him created and brought *actually* to life by a woman. And beneath it we too came alive. We discussed the items that had gone missing from our homes, comically working out how to reunite each one with its rightful owner. Had anyone got an East Coast hat? A Los Angeles sweatshirt? A leopard-print leather belt? Some dungarees? A jumpsuit? A video camera?

'Has anyone seen my pull-up bar?!'

'I have your pull-up bar, holy fuck!'

'No way! I can't do a pull-up so it's still in mint condition!'

'Sisterhood of the travelling pull-up!'

So much perfume had gone missing too, one woman confirming she had seen him with a vast collection of it. 'He said it was for him to mix his original scent.' To which another woman replied, 'I am not sure if narcissistic sociopath is a fragrance you can readily mix.'

Many of these missing items had been gifted to other women, or simply forgotten in their homes. 'I have your jacket!' they wrote. 'He gave me your camera!'

Among the things he had stolen from my home, the most peculiar was a Turkish fruit bowl.

'Do you think now he's found God,' I wrote under the post, 'the holy spirits can guide my fruit bowl back to safety?'

I felt brave with these women around me. I don't doubt we all did. I felt funny again, something I had forgotten how to be, safe enough to laugh at the thing that had devastated me for ten months before.

The fruit bowl continued to be a kind of symbol of joyous relief among us. One woman set up a parody Instagram account of a haggling Turkish fruit-bowl dealer. 'Justice for fruit bowl!' we wrote to each other repeatedly, keeping the joke afloat.

'Wait, doesn't the guy suffer from agoraphobia?'

'It's a wonder he was able to leave the house for long enough to fuck with so many lives!'

'Don't you need to have a house before you can talk about not being able to leave it?'

Speaking of houses: 'Has he brought any of you to chill at another woman's apartment? Maybe saying they were a friend or he was house-sitting? Because he definitely had women in my apartment when I was travelling for work.'

'Um yes. I went to Bergen Street a few times which was a "college friend's" place.'

'Urgh,' another woman replied, 'that was my apartment. He was staying on and off with me for most of this year.'

Away from the public comments, we created a private group chat where we kept on top of it all. One woman compiled a list of his contacts on Facebook. Another from Twitter. Another turned to the mobile payment app Venmo and collected the names of women publicly documented as having given him money there. We tagged them all so they could see the full extent of his actions. Then we contacted dating sites with every email address we knew he used and reported him. By the end of the week, he had been banned from two.

Over the following week, in the privacy of the group chat, we spoke more freely of the things he had done to us. Subgroups branched off – the women in New York in one, the women in London in another, the women in Oslo, and so on. There we spoke about the more nuanced details of it all, and simultaneously kept the main large group chat going with whatever everyone needed to know, or needed to be shared broadly. What I remember of this is that we all listened. We took our turn. We supported each other, with the constant reminder to participate as much or as little as anyone felt comfortable with. We advised each other to duck out of the group and come back later if needed, or not come back at all. We offered details of the things that had helped us heal in the hope it would help someone else. Some women even shared the numbers of their therapists. What was unexpected, throughout, was simply how much we laughed.

What we were learning through our conversations with each other was that there was no evidence of him having had a job for quite some years. He had offered a different employer's name to each woman throughout our simultaneous time with him. There appeared to be only two organisations in the previous years where he had actually worked: one fired him for having a bad attitude; the other had him arrested. No one heard what became of the grand larceny charge, although comments about witnessing his arrest on the shop floor appeared from old colleagues who had also by now come to contribute to the post. His comedy shows were dreadful, lazy, with barely any audience, so there was clearly no money to be made there.

Women were his purpose. We were his purpose.

With only the women who had come forward, it seemed that between 2016 and 2018 alone he had taken nearly $100,000 from them. He had no apartment, no rent, scarcely paid for his own flights or overseas accommodation, food or transport. No doubt the point of the money was to spend it on and seduce women before requesting significant amounts in return, but I believe there was also the thrill of knowing he had taken it. Either way, women were his only livelihood, and the post had jeopardised it all.

Within the month he moved to London. He hastily married the woman he had been referring to as his fiancée.

The post stayed up. And women continued to find it. New women. And we kept the *chain* going.

★

The stories, they were all so similar.

In February 2012 Alyse met *him* on a photoshoot at the technology store where he worked in LA. For six months their relationship was, as she described it, blissful, moving quickly between them, as his love and compliments seemed unending. 'I was absolutely hooked,' Alyse said. 'I was also new to LA, and newly single, so I had no support system close to me. Those first six months were too good to be true— Then I felt crazy, which never ended.'

While he never asked her directly for money, they were by now living together, and she shouldered the financial responsibility of their shared life. Even more so when he lost his job after stealing $70,000 worth of equipment from work, and was arrested in the store. Alyse drove to jail to collect him. Perhaps after this it was too difficult to get another job, or he no longer saw the point in it, but women, it seemed, were more profitable than his other options.

'The progression of amazing to miserable happened very quickly, and the only thing that mattered to me was that I do whatever I can to get back that amazing feeling,' Alyse said. 'He would keep me hanging on with five wonderful days together, followed by two weeks of torture.'

Alyse spiralled into depression, her confidence and sense of self-worth disappeared. She believed she was the problem, losing also her sense of morality and her boundaries as she continuously tried to prove to him that she loved and supported him. 'After the wonderful days together, suddenly I would get the silent treatment. He would leave without saying where he was going, or even that he was going anywhere. He'd ridicule my clothes. Or he'd be laughing and smiling while texting other women constantly, comparing my attitude to other women. He would have phone conversations with friends and talk about me and our relationship as if I wasn't sitting on the couch next to him.'

At the time, while mental health was still a feature in his relationships, he didn't know too much about autism. 'We would watch the TV show *Parenthood* and he seemed intrigued when Ray Romano's character discovered he was autistic. He did tell me once that he was diagnosed with antisocial personality disorder, but said he didn't have the lying characteristic. In fact, he once punched a hole in the wall when we were arguing because I told him, "How will I ever know if you are being honest if you are a sociopath?"

Apparently, that word made him furious and he yelled at me that he's not one.'

Alyse met with his mother on some occasions, both in her home in Atlanta and when she visited them in LA. He had told Alyse that his mother was a high priestess. 'He said she had cervical cancer, and that if she died he wouldn't miss her.'

They stayed together for two and a half years, during which time Alyse had become pregnant twice. Both times she had an abortion. As always, women's pain was not something he cared much for. Which he also made clear when she had a kidney infection. 'I was in tremendous pain, peeing blood every ten minutes and I couldn't sleep. In the middle of the night, he walked about a mile to the American pharmacy CVS to get me medicine. When he came home I thanked him over and over again. I genuinely felt so loved by him. And then he told me that the sooner I felt better, the sooner he could fuck me again.'

Finally, she went through his computer, desperate to find anything concrete she could use against him in the break-up. She found a vast number of photographs of naked women and evidence that he had slept with someone she knew and trusted.

They separated, and Alyse was diagnosed with panic disorder, depression and PTSD.

When the Instagram post took off, his friends sent her the link to it. 'In a way I felt like it was therapy for me to help other women directly involved with him, because I knew his stories, and I knew for a fact he was not to be trusted.'

In October 2014 Jenny met *him* on OkCupid while he was staying in east London. He talked a lot on their first date, which had suited her, his stories both fun and fascinating. When he was a child, he had said, while misbehaving in a shop, the owner brought his hand gently down on his head and immediately calmed him. His mother looked startled; this shop owner, who was also a Japanese martial arts instructor, agreed to tutor him, providing the discipline that the child so badly needed. His mother, he told Jenny, was a drug dealer and she gave her son to this man most nights of the week to train him. Alone, he travelled by bus to the man's martial arts school, where he spent hours at a time. At seventeen he went to Japan to study Weng Chun, judo and other martial art forms with his master, living there for two years and becoming an expert in martial arts. His stories, it seemed, always positioned him as someone who was traditional and hard-working, and, above all else, someone who truly valued discipline, which he extended to monogamy and family life.

'On our first date,' Jenny said, 'he asked me things like how many kids did I want. His reply was often *me too*! He built up this image of the kind of dad he would be – one of those dads that has one strapped to their back and front. With me having the other two. Like I was someone he could see himself with.'

In the beginning he paid for their dates and took her shopping, while he stayed in a London hotel for over a month. Then he left for Zurich where he said he was working as a sound engineer. He quickly returned to London to be with Jenny, he claimed. Now, without a job in Zurich, he no longer had money and needed to live with her rent-free. 'At first it was this wonderful whirlwind romance, staying at his hotel and going out to restaurants and bars. But once he was staying at mine it became draining. He stayed home watching TV all day, and would lift his luggage up and down as a "workout". He paid me little attention and didn't listen to the things I wanted to talk about. He talked about himself nonstop. I did all the cooking. I drove us everywhere.'

The compliments and affection that had been so present in the first month had by this point totally disappeared. Now, staying in her flat, he was a different man. 'He once told me I was fat, and he laughed a few times at what I wore. I often felt on edge, like I might say the wrong thing, or not keep up with how smart he said he was. He would spend long periods on his phone, and packed and repacked his suitcase every day. I felt invisible.'

Jenny tried to find him work but nothing ever seemed to come of it. 'Then he said he couldn't work in London without a visa, so we should get married to make this happen.'

Thankfully, they never did. And in January 2015 he went back to Zurich and failed to contact Jenny often. 'He posted a picture on Instagram of himself with a supposed stab wound. I tried to call him to see if he was okay, but he would never pick up and only messaged to say he was on a train. I asked him where he was going but just got vague replies. He was really rude all of the time, so I told him it had to be over.'

In May 2015, Olivia met him on OkCupid. Her roommate had recently moved out, and so it happened that *he* was spending more and more time at her New York apartment. She enjoyed it. She liked having a kind and committed man who she cared about around the house and so, like this, he moved in with her. He cleaned her apartment regularly, took her out on dates which he paid for, and was keen to spend time with her friends. Then, two months later, it all changed. The dates stopped, and so did the sex and affection. Now, no longer wanting to go out with Olivia's friends, he started to tell her he was agoraphobic.

'In these early stages, when he was still very good to me, he called it "leaving nuts and berries",' Olivia said. 'Like it was something he was doing to lure me in. I thought he was joking.'

Once the romance stopped, he immediately began asking for money. He had lost his job, he said, and needed some to get by until he began the high-paying job he was just on the cusp of starting. 'As soon as you give him money he tries to get as much out of you in one go as he can.' Olivia gave him most of the $5,000 he had taken from her, in three instalments. 'He had positioned himself as a hard-working person who was about to get a good job, and could pay it all back.'

As time went on Olivia grew more and more miserable in the relationship, but there was never the right time to leave him because of all the bad things that repeatedly happened to him. 'Suddenly his mum got super sick,' Olivia said, familiarly, 'and he had to go to Atlanta on a moment's notice.'

By December 2015, life, he said, had got even worse. 'He went to Tennessee because his friend had shot his daughter, then shot himself. Then his other daughter tried to kill herself and was braindead in hospital.' I remembered a version of this story too, when I had been pregnant and exhausted. 'From Tennessee,' Olivia said, 'he went to Canada because his ex-girlfriend, the one who had died in an accident – her mum was now dying of cancer.' Many of us had been given a description of this elusive past girlfriend, too – the only woman he had loved before us. They had lived in Canada together ten years earlier, and she had died in a car crash, he said, while he was driving the car. In some versions she was pregnant with his child.

By early 2016 he had stopped going home to Olivia altogether. 'He was either sleeping at a friend's house, or at the hospital, or coming home really late from a comedy show after I had already gone to work. He always had some reason for it.'

Nearly a year after their first meeting he began to tell Olivia about his serious health problems. 'He was at a bunch of clinics and they were studying his brain because he was losing his mind. He said he was getting electric shocks, and they were injecting chemicals into his spine, then making it move around with lasers.'

Olivia, like many of us, spent most of her time worried about him, paralysed by the endless disorders that were plaguing him and their relationship. 'I would actively choose to believe him. Because as it got more and more, it got too horrible to think about the alternative.'

In June 2016, around the time I met him, she ended it. 'I broke up with him over text because he was never at home and I never saw him. He moved his stuff out the next day.' Olivia moved to Chicago for a job, but they stayed in touch. 'He would send these long poetic, sweet messages. Looking back on it I can see why I chose to believe it all.' She returned to New York for a visit in January 2017. 'My flight home got cancelled,' she told me, 'because there was a snowstorm.'

I think about that snowstorm. I think about the snow. Often. How he had meant to be in Atlanta during that time, the night his mother died. How I was held in place by the solidity of it all.

'He invited me to a show he was doing,' Olivia said. 'I went to meet him in Midtown in a blizzard. Then, as soon as I got off the train, he texted to say he was actually elsewhere and I should go there instead. Then he stopped responding to my messages.' Olivia gave up and went back to where she was staying. 'Then I saw pictures on Facebook a week later, and he was just at that show all along, the original one that I was standing outside of, in the snow, waiting for him.'

In April 2017, still a few months before the post fully erupted, Olivia had seen him allude to being suicidal on his social media. Having not heard from him, she searched his name on Instagram to see if anyone had posted anything about his wellbeing. What she found instead was Zoe's post. At that time there were no comments from other women, only the caption by Zoe calling him a psychopath and warning others. Olivia texted him, and this time he replied immediately. His message was long and full of what he considered to be an explanation, but what came across as odd ramblings. Soon after, he sent her several screenshots about psychopathy.

She kept an eye on the post and in November 2017, when many, many more women arrived, Olivia had been waiting for it. Finally, when it happened, her feelings towards it were complex: 'In all of this, there's a lot of excitement and good feelings in being able to connect with everybody. To feel supported and not crazy, to not feel like it's my fault. But there's this other really dark part that wants to measure myself against everyone else, and really learn about everybody else's details of their stories, so that I can think about the nuances of my specific experience and how it played out worse or better.'

I knew this to be true in myself. How I had heard about the many lovely dates and the way he had helped some women around the house, and I had felt jealous. I too had used the slight differences in our interactions with him as a way to measure my own worth. Society had already taught me to do this, and he had compounded this further in his relationships with us.

In April 2016 Eleanor met him on Tinder in New York. Their relationship was casual during the first eight months and the time they spent together was infrequent, but they remained in fairly regular contact over the phone.

His mother, he had told Eleanor, had blood cancer, which he used to explain his repeated absence as he travelled back and forth to Atlanta to be with her.

In December 2016, when I was pregnant, he turned it on more strongly with Eleanor, wanting to see more of her. He asked for a spare key to her apartment, slowly taking over more and more of his things.

By January 2017 Eleanor was looking to move apartments. He had a good friend, he said, who lived in a building in Bed-Stuy. He pulled up the address and showed her rental photos online. A few days before the blizzard, a week before I went to the clinic, he sent Eleanor to the building to have a look around, insisting she take the apartment that was free. The building, Eleanor realised a year later, was mine.

In January 2017, just as he had vanished from my life, he began asking her for money. 'It started with him generally being broke,' she said, 'but he ramped it up when he said he had been diagnosed with spots on his brain, which was causing him to need medical attention and hospital treatment. Whenever I gave him money it came with desperate pleas, saying he was struggling and in pain.' He repeatedly reassured Eleanor that it was a loan. That he had prospective payouts coming from freelance work he had done on film sets, or a court case involving his previous employers who had screwed him over. Eleanor gave him just over $9,000.

'I was so excited and happy that I'd met someone who seemed really interesting. But as time went on it always felt like I was waiting for something. For him to get a job, to have some money, to get treatment, for us both to be travelling less, for us to spend more time together. I definitely spent a lot of the relationship feeling unhappy and worrying about him. Deep down I always knew something wasn't right, but he had manipulated me to a point where my desire to make it work with him was stronger than the doubt I had, so I let myself believe in something that wasn't real.'

When the Instagram post took off Eleanor was still in a relationship with him. 'It ended because I saw Zoe's post. I hadn't seen much of him for a while because he had a list of excuses, including being in Atlanta with his dying mother. I hadn't really engaged with his social media much, but I hadn't heard a lot from him and was curious to see what was going on. I guess he had blocked me on Instagram, so when I searched for him only the hashtag of his name came up instead of his account, and that led to Zoe's post.'

Shocked, Eleanor didn't reach out to him, and when she heard from him a few days later she couldn't bring herself to reply. 'He must have realised then that I had seen it and he sent apologies and excuses which pretty much amounted to what he posted in the comments to everyone.'

As surreal as it was, ironically, it was something Eleanor could finally make sense of. 'I felt like the bottom just fell out of everything. It was all so crazy and such a betrayal of trust. But it also explained his behaviour in a much more believable way than the stories he had spun to me. In a weird way it felt like a spell had been broken.'

In January 2017 Kay started speaking to him on Tinder, before meeting him at a comedy show sometime later. She hadn't been looking for anything serious, but he was, as usual, quick to introduce the idea of commitment.

'He provided the antidote to dating in New York,' Kay said. In a transient city where it wasn't uncommon to schedule three different social plans in one evening, relationships played out much the same way. 'He told me he wasn't like that and you think, *Thank God!* Because dating in New York is so fucked up.' It was easy to find a date in New York because, it seemed, most people were single, and single is exactly how so many men wanted to remain. It was unusual to meet a man like *him*, one who spoke of wanting to get to know a woman first, and love her, and commit. This pretence caught Kay as much as it had the rest of us.

'He talked a lot. He just fucking talked, constantly.' Kay laughed. 'And he told me he was depressed immediately. I suffer from depression, so I don't look down on it. But we didn't go out again after that first night, which he said was because of his mental health. Everything else happened indoors.'

He asked Kay for a key to her apartment, telling her it would help alleviate his depression. She refused to give him one. Then he told her he had a huge hospital bill to pay, and needed money for his medication.

'I had just sold my house in Philadelphia,' Kay said. 'This was literally the only time in my life I had excess money in the bank. The timing was so unfortunate. He kept talking about how he was in a bad way and I thought, people have taken care of me in my life when I've not had money. The amount of times I've picked pennies out of my couch – I thought it would be good karma to help, to give to somebody who was just like someone I had also been.'

But, as with all of the women, Kay's gut was telling her something different: 'I remember writing him a cheque and being like, "I'm going to go with you." Because there was a part of me that was like . . . I knew. I knew. And he came out with a lot of excuses about it being private and how I should let him do it himself.' Kay had given him $2,000.

'At that point, my abandonment issues kicked in,'

Kay said honestly. 'That's my part in this. I ended up writing him the cheque despite my better judgement, because I was worried if I didn't write that cheque he would leave. This is so embarrassing to admit, but I really thought if I gave him the money he would see I was good and lovable. As soon as he left the house with the cheque I had intense panic. My system knew. My body knew. But my brain didn't want to.'

He disappeared for a few weeks to work in Finland, he told her, and when he returned she collected him from the airport. But soon he disappeared again. 'He told me his mum was dying and he had to be in Atlanta a lot. Then he would show up at mine from the airport with no bags, but he had an answer for everything.'

During the months they spent together he invited her to his place. He was living in an apartment that belonged to an old college buddy who was out of town for a while. The apartment, Kay thought, didn't feel like a man's apartment but she didn't think too much of it. 'He was taking me to Eleanor's apartment,' Kay said. 'One day he just picked up this camera from another room and said it was his and I should have it. It was Eleanor's. Now I know the whole place was Eleanor's.'

At some point he got very drunk with Kay who, still uneasy about the money she had given him, made him sign a piece of paper agreeing to pay her back. 'He broke up with me within twenty-four hours of that.'

Looking for answers she searched for him on

Instagram. He had blocked her from his account and the only thing that came up was Zoe's post. 'I was broken. I was suicidal. I felt this love and then it was all a lie. It was all an act. I felt like I was in a play, but I was an unwilling participant in that play. Who could act like that? I felt like I didn't want to live like this.'

She arranged to speak with Zoe on the phone, who told Kay she had not been the first woman to get in touch, and wouldn't be the last. 'I felt ashamed, and silly. But I knew it was much more than just me being naive and vulnerable. But my friends didn't understand that, nobody really could. And then, finally, there were all these women telling their stories. And finally they all understood.'

In March 2017 Samantha met him in a restaurant near her Manhattan apartment, after speaking to him on Tinder. 'When he walked in, he said, *I saw you at the door and almost turned around. I thought, why would she want to date someone like me?*' He had always been good at this – the self-deprecation, the gratitude to have met you, while immediately setting the tone as someone insecure. 'That night he asked the waitress, *Do you think this is a first date, or does it look like we've been together for years?*' I too remembered this about him – how he introduced the idea of a loving cemented relationship long before you even had a chance to decide for yourself. Later that night in the cab he put his hand on hers, and took a photograph of it.

After that they spend every day together. They went on regular dates and took long walks comfortably around her neighbourhood. Agoraphobia wasn't a feature for him in their relationship. Presumably there were no other women he was dating in her area. At first his mental health was only slightly present. He had mentioned occasionally having depression, and only vaguely referred to 'being on the spectrum', perhaps because he knew Samantha worked closely with children who had autism and the lie wouldn't fit so easily.

He met regularly with her sister and her friends, and paid for their dates and her groceries. He was attentive and loving and keen to be a part of Samantha's life. By April he was staying with her every night and had brought many of his things to her apartment. Samantha remembered that he spent a lot of money during this period, buying himself clothes and shoes most days from high-end brands. She thought nothing of it. It seemed he had a successful job during the day, while doing comedy shows in the evenings. 'He'd say he had a show that finished at 11 p.m. and then he'd always be home by midnight or 1 a.m. I never questioned him. He didn't stand me up, and was always there for me. As far as I was concerned I had met the man I was going to marry.'

A couple of months into their relationship, however, he disappeared. It was sudden and he got in touch to say he was in New Jersey for work, and barely contacted her for some time after. Annoyed, she messaged him:

'I said, "If this is your way of pushing me away, congratulations, it worked. I want my keys back."' He was, he said, abroad and would be there for a while. This was the first Samantha had heard of him leaving the US.

'On the date he was meant to return, suddenly his mum was dying, and he had to go straight to Atlanta instead to be with her,' Samantha said. By now, his mental health issues, he claimed, had also worsened and he needed money to help with them. Samantha began to send it to him.

By the end of June, Samantha hadn't seen him for two months. He messaged to say he had finally returned from Atlanta to New York and would catch a train to be with her and her family in the Hamptons in time for dinner. He didn't show. 'The next day I remember feeling the worst feeling inside of me. I ran to the ocean and just jumped into it because I literally didn't know what was going on inside my mind. I just wanted to escape.' By the time she returned he had messaged her, frantically, telling her that things had gotten bad with his mother again, and he didn't feel stable. 'He was telling me that he was sitting by his mother's hospital bed and holding her hand. I thought if my mum was dying maybe I would be behaving like him too.'

He began asking for more money to help with his medication, now saying he was in an even worse way. She gave it to him, before buying him a bus ticket to meet her family in New Hampshire. He didn't show up for that either. Now he was starting to say that going to the movies gave him a headache, getting on a bus gave him a headache.

By August, Samantha hadn't seen him since May; he was still claiming he was mostly in Atlanta with his mother. 'He kept saying he'd come back and I'd open the door one day and he'd be sitting there. I opened my door every day after work thinking he'd be there and it was just so depressing. This emptiness in my stomach when each time he wasn't there.'

Samantha's depression and anxiety were increasing and finally she could take no more. 'I lost it. And he sent me this whole diatribe about how selfish I was. I stopped replying to him, and I think that threw him.' Soon after, he messaged her again, this time apologising, insisting that he just needed to spend his mother's final days with her and soon he and Samantha would be able to start their lives properly together. But by then she didn't feel the same urgency to save the relationship. 'Before, I think that's what I was trying to do the whole time: If I give him this, it will just go back to this really nice thing that we had. If I give him this, it's what he needs to get back on his feet and we can get back to what had been so special.'

Now, Samantha saw things differently. In the space of a few months, she had given him thousands of dollars and she'd had enough. 'I told him I couldn't do this anymore.' He messaged saying he was on the plane from Atlanta to New York and would be going straight to her apartment in a few hours to see her. Again, he didn't show. The next morning, he checked himself into a clinic. He said his doctors had said he wasn't stable enough for a relationship, but he wanted to remain friends. Samantha agreed.

A few weeks later he messaged again and finally came to her apartment. 'He cried hysterically. Nonstop crying. And he was telling me how much he loves me. But he was saying a million things. And that's what he does – just creates so much confusion.'

The following day she returned from work and he was still in her apartment. He claimed that his doctors said it was okay if they lived together, and he should move in. 'I just thought, "this is so wrong".'

He was still asking Samantha for money, but now she refused. Samantha had given him close to $9,000 since May. He pleaded that his health insurance wouldn't kick in until September. 'I said, "Well, figure it out, I'm not giving you money." He was like, what the hell am I supposed to do?'

When it became clear she had stopped giving him money for good he told her it was over. He said they couldn't be together; couldn't work on their relationship or start a life together as he was going to a mental hospital in Vermont. 'I asked him what the place is called. He said the name wasn't important as I wouldn't be able to visit him. He said he was also considering going to one in the UK, but he couldn't tell me the name for that one either.'

Then, one day, as she was scrolling through Twitter

she saw him making plans to go to Berlin with his brother for New Year. 'I was like, how are you online when you're meant to be in a mental hospital? He said they let him have an iPad for half an hour.' By now furious he was making holiday plans while owing her money, she brought it up with him. 'I asked him about getting my money back and he said that his doctors had told him to block me. I was apparently driving him into psychosis and he had a harassment order against me. He said I was *agitating a mentally ill individual* and that the police had it on record.'

Samantha blocked his number. But he still found her on WhatsApp and continued to message her there. 'He said he was giving up his citizenship but would be in New York once a month and wanted to see me on those days. I said all I want is my money back. Again, he claimed I was being nasty and agitating his mental health, when he was just trying to mend things.'

In October he messaged her again, claiming he was sleeping on the streets, trying to pull her back in. 'I didn't respond.'

During their time together he had told Samantha he didn't have an Instagram account. The reality is he had pre-emptively blocked her from the very beginning. But Samantha had a friend who knew some of his friends, and in mid-October her friend saw he had been tagged in a photograph with those men. Samantha's friend clicked on his account and his Instagram page opened up. There were numerous photographs of the woman who later became his wife. 'I was in a Chase bank when I saw it,' Samantha said, 'and I literally sat down on the floor. Throughout all the bullshit I never even suspected another woman.'

She messaged him immediately, telling him that she knew everything, wanted her money back, and that he would be hearing from her lawyer. 'His first response was to tell me to go away. He told me he had never wanted me and claimed I was jealous that he had chosen her over me. I said I just wanted my money. He told me it was too late. And then he wished me luck trying to get it back.'

In November 2017 Samantha was still furious and wanted more answers. She searched for his name on Instagram and, still blocked, only Zoe's post came up. At that time there were only three comments on it. Zoe's warning to other women was prominent, and Samantha wrote her own comment, confirming what Zoe said was all true. Zoe messaged her privately to say that by then twenty women had messaged her directly. Samantha commented again, with more detail, and so it all began.

Samantha also reached out to the woman he was about to marry. She told her everything he had done and sent screenshots of their recent conversations. They messaged each other back and forth, but the woman was really dismissive. 'The way she wrote the messages sounded exactly like how *he* talks.' Samantha thought she was speaking to him and not his fiancée, that he was in total control of her account. This resonated with something Jessica had once told me, how she had eventually gone into her settings on Facebook and seen a lot of women she didn't know pre-emptively blocked from her account, and we wondered if the same were happening here.

In the days that followed, when the post fully erupted, when all of the women came forward, so much of the depression and suicidal ideations Samantha had been feeling lifted. 'I had felt dumb, ashamed, silly. But it had been so much more for me than just being someone who was naive. And seeing all these stories — that helped. I got to see that you are all strong, smart and successful women. You're all pretty great people. And I felt better for that.'

Alone, we had become the lies he had told us. Together, we were learning to unravel them. We were building the *chain*. We were learning to replace him with ourselves.

iv.

Do men find life so full of humour and
    joy
That for want of excitement they smash
    up the toy?
      — *Amy Lowell, 'A Ballad of Footmen'*

When the vast sexual misconduct in Hollywood was revealed publicly, women everywhere felt the *chain* and spoke out about their own experiences. This was not a witch-hunt against men, as many saw it. There was no mass hysteria spurred by imaginary dangers, as happened in the Basque, Salem or Torsåker witch trials. Men rape – that much is fact. Men touch, and hit, and they kill women. Men abandon their pregnant girlfriends, whether at a clinic or after a baby is born. They manipulate and emotionally torture them. These are not accusations of the supernatural – these are truths, basic everyday realities. Caught-out men talk of 'witch-hunts' against them, because where there is no precedent of men fleeing institutional tyranny by women there can only be the borrowed language from the persecution they themselves impose.

Those of our sisters who are no longer physically here to share their stories still do so by belonging to the *chain*. Those who were truly hunted, accused of being witches, were the women who expressed interest in their own sexual fulfilment; women who were unable to save others from sickness; women who inherited financial security; the women who stood out. These women were not possessed, they were simply existing in the many ways we do. And our own abuser had seen these very same qualities in us as our own crimes.

★

Mythology tells us there are men, and there are monsters. Yet, brutality does not belong to the practice of mythical creatures, but to mortals.

With this in mind, one of the most conflicting celebrity sexual misconduct allegations to come out of the MeToo movement was the one levelled at the comedian Aziz Ansari. It was, to my memory, the most divisive account, the one that split men and women on the definitions of both assault and personal responsibility. Ansari had taken his date to dinner, then back to his house. He had made moves on her (as we understand it) that she reciprocated. And then she had told him she would actually prefer to have sex on their second date. He poured her a glass of wine, handed it to her, and asked if that counted. Maybe he meant it to be cute. But during the thirty minutes his date spent with him at his home she says she repeatedly moved her hands away from his genitals when he put them there, went cold and stopped kissing him back, kept walking away from him as he followed her around the apartment, sticking his fingers into her mouth. She told him she didn't 'want to feel forced', to which his response seemed understanding, before 'he sat back and pointed to his penis and motioned for me to go down on him'. She says she did, then called an Uber, and went home in tears. Ansari has since said in a Netflix comedy special that he felt scared and humiliated, and 'terrible that this person felt this way', to loud applause. He has also said in a statement that he believed the encounter was consensual, but he had taken her words to heart.

I did not read the details of Ansari's night and wonder on the definitions of assault. I have answered enough phone calls, as sleep beckons, to crying friends journeying home. The men who rely on the *assumption* of consent. Who treat us as though we don't need to give further permission for sex if we've already permitted going back to theirs, invited them to ours, kissed them, got into bed with them, consented to sex with them once before, married them even. Expectation is waved around as though it's legislation. *But you're already here! I'm hard now, though! Don't leave me hanging with blue balls! I'm just going to kiss you, nothing else! You just have to touch it, that's all!*

Insisting someone changes their answer from a 'no' does not eventually add up to a 'yes': when he persists that her staying is easier than going home; when he ignores just how drunk she is; when he takes advantage of a woman's depression as much as her drunkenness . . .

In fact, I don't think we talk enough about women's relationship with sex when they are depressed, or traumatised: about how common it is for women to rely on multiple partners in these situations. About where the line blurs between a woman's sexual agency, and the men who depend on how she is being governed by her own distress: chasing emotional hits, or too exhausted to fight back, or simply too full of self-loathing to believe she deserves any better. Predators understand the power dynamic; with a fan, with an employee, with a woman walking home, with a woman throwing up outside a bar, with a woman consumed by her own despair.

I have lived and witnessed the spectrum to know where Ansari falls on it. But not everyone knows. There are women, too, who perhaps have not sat at a busy table of girlfriends reciting such encounters, so are unaware we have been classifying all along. Would we even be able to refine the definitions of assault and abuse if there wasn't a communal catalogue being held by women? Women who hold these men accountable, when police and jurors and society won't.

We hold on to every experience in the hope we'll know who and what to avoid in the future, to warn other women too, so the *chain* provides us with the confidence to say, 'I believe her, because it happened to us too.'

Still, if Ansari's actions were harassment and not merely flirty perseverance, didn't that mean a lot of men have been guilty of coercion and assault at some point? The terrifying answer – for everyone involved – is yes. More than likely.

And to agree that Ansari's actions were abusive would mean an admission of guilt for far too many. It would mean a confession to actions crueller than the average person believes they are capable of. It would also require an admission from women not yet ready to acknowledge they are capable of being abused.

Harvey Weinstein was offered to us as the brutish villain personified, a gluttonous fiend in an ill-fitting, gaping bathrobe, grotesque in contrast to the beautiful, fair young women he molested. Bill Cosby, the once family-man father-figure who betrayed a nation when allegations were made of him dragging women through his Beverly Hills mansion. Jeffrey Epstein, the wealthy elite and merciless child catcher.

But Harvey Weinstein is not a monster, though we may have understood him to have acted as one. He is a man, as much as Bill Cosby, as much as Jeffrey Epstein. That is to say – their actions may not be comprehensible, but the framework of manhood from which they work is. This is where the floor fell from beneath us. An excess of power allowed these men's abuse to reach such extreme levels, but men – regular men – exploit their authority over women at work too, they date-rape women in bars as well, they dominate and silence inexperienced, vulnerable girls.

Bad people assault. Good people assault. Both are possible in a world where language and action have not quite fully collided. We have been told that these things happen in blackened alleyways in the dead of night; they break into the bedrooms of women they don't know; a wicked stranger reaching into the darkness and dragging a woman from it. Many sleep well knowing this is not them.

But the reality is, assault is likely to resemble Ansari's interaction much more closely than anything involving beasts lurking in bushes. So it is possible that a man believes he was good to his partner, but has still raped them. It is possible a man, upon never hearing the word 'no' from his date, did not understand what is entailed for a meaningful 'yes'.

All around us, people were speaking about being harassed and abused throughout their life. Yet it seemed there were barely any abusers.

Men, it seemed, supported the MeToo movement when the perpetrators were far removed from average life. This was Hollywood, and we were all watching another movie. But as the accounts began to hit closer to home, so did the objections. Were women now being too sensitive? Were women attention-seekers wanting in on the status quo? Were women now trying to cancel men they simply didn't like? Were we making it unsafe for a man to say he found a woman attractive? How were men meant to talk to a woman now? How could he tell her she was beautiful, ask for her number, engage in 'harmless' banter in the office or pub? Were we going too far?

As we understood it Weinstein was a power-wielding maniacal abuser; Ansari was just a guy on a bad date. After all, what is receiving oral sex from a woman who is already naked, who entered the apartment of her own accord, who does not throw a punch and leave, if not consensual? This question was being asked across newsrooms and homes alike. But to understand that men manipulate women for sex, for control, means to also recognise that women are frightened to disappoint men, and it is this combination that acts as a gateway to abuse.

The conversation about Ansari was as much about what leads a woman into this space, as it was about the man.

I had seen this with my own relationships, and in my relationship with *him*. I hadn't given *him* any money, but I understood why the other women had, because I too had allowed my own boundaries to be crossed in so many ways. Some women do this with sex, with their bodies, or care, not asking for what they want, not complaining when something hurts. Because we wanted these men to be grateful for us, to keep loving us, to stay. The honest truth is, even I didn't fully understand what abuse was. I was looking for the monsters. Not the average, everyday derisive behaviours, which is part of why I couldn't see I too was being abused.

★

As the historical witch trials against women took place, many confessed to crimes they had not committed. Many of us still do. We plead guilty to not having been enough, to not being beautiful or slim or smart enough, not white enough, too successful, not successful enough, too vocal, not vocal at all. Had we been better mothers – even in the absence of children – perhaps we would have spared ourselves the heat beneath our feet. I was never bound to a stake. But I know what it means to be punished for the possession of my own body.

Some years ago I watched from the audience as a well-known comedian told a joke about rape. I walked out, as many people have in these situations. I was not upset. Rather, I felt a peculiar kind of boredom. If I am no longer surprised that men rape, why then would it shock me to know they laugh about it?

The irritant was not whatever thought he had on the matter – too unremarkable to now remember – but that he had wanted to say it at all. I have spent enough time on stage to know this space is used as an invisibility cloak for raw truth. In those early years of being a spoken-word artist we riffed distracting witticisms offstage, then spoke honestly up on it. Where I had laughed joyously and drunk cheap whisky and Cokes with the crowd, it had been behind a microphone where I processed heartbreak. I was not the light-hearted person that I seemed offstage. I was consumed by sadness and that was my truth.

I enjoyed those days. Yet, I never heard a poem performed by a man who lyrically talked an audience through his furious disappointment with women and didn't mean it. They recited rhapsodic preachings for women to have less sex. They recorded poems that shamed abortions, and suggested that losing your virginity too soon was a suicide, or HIV waiting to happen. They blamed women for not knowing when a man cheated, or for being the reason he did. And they posted it all online too, as though the stage had not been enough. 'If you're a bad bitch,' one verse went, 'don't be surprised when the RSPCA in me decides to put you down.'

These were my first days of understanding. These were not performances, they were admissions.

Even in the days before Louis C.K. was accused of performing non-consensual masturbation in front of women – for which he has since apologised – the debut film he wrote had eyebrows raised. It didn't help that he played a guy who idolises a film director based on Woody Allen, or that a character pleasures himself in front of a woman at work. In one scene a young actor reveals his genitals to a woman driving in a car with him. 'I gotta take it out,' the character tells her. When Louis C.K. repeated jokes in his stand-up and TV shows about masturbation it seemed obsessive, because it was.

R. Kelly sang untiringly about his fixation and horrifying sexual compulsions on 'Bump N' Grind', 'Down Low' – and on and on it went. And perhaps the most haunting lyrics he'd written: 'Age ain't nothing but a number, throwing down ain't nothing but a thing . . .' It's these lyrics that he gave to a fourteen-year-old Aaliyah to sing back to him, a child he was already having 'sex' with, and like this he made her a star. The song became a hit and teenage girls repeated the lyrics out loud as Kelly, then twenty-seven, went on to marry Aaliyah when she was just fifteen.

Kelly continued to tell on himself in 'I Like the Crotch on You', 'Home Alone', 'If I'm Wit' You', 'Wanna Be There' and, perhaps the most telling of all, 'I Admit' ('I admit I fuck with all the ladies, that's both older and young ladies, but tell me how they call it pedophile because of that shit').

While Kelly was raping underage girls, and locking women up in his mansion, his live shows continued to be intensely pornographic. He thrust himself at an audience dominated by young girls. He called teenagers on stage to serenade them with exactly what he wanted to do to them. His perversions were heartlessly cruel and on full display.

When Kanye West and Kim Kardashian broke up, Kanye bought the house opposite, unwilling to give her any space or privacy in her single life. He dedicated his Instagram to posting screenshots of their private texts and pleaded for his millions of fans to make Kim get back with him. Most alarmingly, he sent her a truck brimming with red roses on Valentine's Day, which looked disturbingly like a hearse. Perhaps because it was meant to, as the same visual appeared again in Kanye's music video where he kidnaps and decapitates an effigy of Kim's then new boyfriend, comedian Pete Davidson.

In a documentary about Jimmy Savile's inconceivable perverse degeneracy – the paedophilia, rape and necrophilia – decades of interviews with him demonstrated this was a man who had no intention to stop telling you who he was. On the panel of a popular British comedy show, when queried on what he does living in a caravan he responds, 'Anybody I can lay my hands on' – to applause.

When asked in an interview if he runs marathons because he is trying to punish himself, he replies, 'The only time you punish yourself is when you are with young ladies. Then you punish yourself because you're such a villain. You should be kind to them, and you're not kind to them. And you squeeze them and make them go "Ouch!"'

In other footage he is shown making ceaseless sexual advances towards the female host of one of the most watched breakfast shows, something he does to her live on television for years. At one point he tells her, 'I'm looking forward to getting a job when I'm sixty-five. Maybe a caretaker in a girls' school.' In a different interview he tells a woman, 'I might be jumping off things and kidnapping local ladies. Because I live in Glencoe, and we rustle cattle up there, and we also kidnap ladies and sell them.' These are all dispersed between throwaway remarks about getting prison time if he were to share all of his anecdotes, and the repeated quip, 'My case comes up next Thursday!'

And yet, perhaps the most harrowing, most provoking admissions are not even about what he does, but what he knows he can. 'I never ever thought that I was clever,' Savile says. 'Tricky, yes. I'm a very tricky fella. If you are clever, you can slip up. You never slip up if you're tricky.' In fact, it seemed so much had been structured around trickiness. When asked what he was most afraid of losing, the answer was a simple one: 'Freedom.' He says, 'I've got the freedom to do pretty well anything now. You don't know. You are constrained by certain things. I'm not in your world. I'm not constrained by pretty well anything. I'm alone in the world now. But I'm quite happy because I borrow everybody else. I borrow their joys, I borrow their sorrows.'

Realistically these men were all able to hide in plain sight or, rather, play out their fantasies publicly and undeterred because of who their targets were. C.K.'s victims weren't considered funny enough or well-known enough comedians to warrant fans of C.K. losing access to his shows over. Kelly's were Black girls and Black women who are still, and historically, the most forgotten, erased and under-cared-for demographic. This lends itself tragically to everything from being at disproportionate risk of sexual assault to Black women's medical pain being misunderstood or ignored by doctors and healthcare professionals alike. Kanye's casualty was a woman the world loves to hate for being famous and rich from a leaked sex tape, for being known for her sexuality and body. Savile's victims were young girls – they were children – and the vulnerable, people with disabilities and psychiatric issues, none of whom were considered useful or to have made a beneficial contribution to society compared to the venerated men who are told they offer so much more.

Women didn't matter. No matter how rich or beautiful. Women weren't safe. No matter how old or young. No matter how vulnerable. And our abusers were telling us every way they could.

★

In the months that followed the clinic I found myself listening to clips of *his* stand-up routines. I had been in a relationship with a man I believed to be one way and I needed to know the other.

He posted recordings from his comedy shows to YouTube, he uploaded podcasts of conversations with ex-girlfriends and, more bizarrely, Uber drivers who he talks candidly with about how awful he finds women, how easy he finds us to manipulate.

At a comedy night filmed a few blocks from my Brooklyn apartment, only two months after the clinic, he is disengaged and shirty with his audience, picking on them sporadically. He comments on one man: 'If he's from England – you guys don't use condoms, you guys aren't circumcised, you kind of twist-tie that little tip, and let it out later.' Condoms, or the lack of, feature heavily throughout his shows. You are pushed to find one set that doesn't see him bragging on stage about the men who don't use them. 'I lived in Shoreditch for a long time,' he continues. 'I might have kids, I dunno, I don't live out there. What am I gonna do? Raise them? I don't do it here.'

A story he goes on to tell about his time in Amsterdam feels about as authentic as his mother's constant rising from the dead. Outdated, banal scenarios of twenty-quid hookers and heroin in bars. Then a convoluted story about wearing a Transformers T-shirt and going home with a woman, who he is having sex with when the condom breaks. 'I gotta tell her. I'm like, "Hey, listen. Wake up—"' The men in the room laugh. He pauses for them to enjoy it. The story continues with him putting the morning-after pill in her cheese, comparing her to a dog forced to take its medicine, holding its mouth tight and shut. He raises his hand to his face to demonstrate covering the mouth of an animal, or woman. The joke he is telling shifts here to an awkward conversation between himself and this woman he has slept with, who confused his Transformers T-shirt as showing support for trans people, as it is revealed here that she is.

I am unsure what reaction he was after, but he gets none from the audience. His tone shifts immediately, harshly punctuating his final words, an angry and defensive attack on how he wants equality but that doesn't include 'the gays'. The woman in his story asks if he is upset that she 'used to be a dude'. No, he tells her flippantly, he was so high on drugs it was likely to happen anyway. What he's actually angry about, he tells her, is that he wasted a condom to begin with. 'I could have gone into that shit raw.'

★

Two years later at a comedy club in Sweden, he tells his audience, 'I was a player before I met my wife. Obviously if you're this *fine*, this is what happens. I don't know what women were expecting to get from me. On the positive side, you can get some dick, maybe. Other than that, I'm gonna run your credit cards up. And they tried to warn my wife, "No, don't be with him because he's a player!" This one girl bought me a plane ticket to see her, which I didn't ask for. But I went to see other women instead.' A man's booming laugh can be heard at this point. 'She was upset about that for a while. Couple of other girls would be like, "Hey, I'm gonna get you an Uber after your show, you can come to my house." Cool! Uber driver, take me to this *other* address cos this *other* girl is way finer. And it wasn't like there weren't warning signs. Because I have a podcast that I do, and it's me talking to my ex-girlfriends about how terrible I was. You listened to it, you thought it was a joke?'

The reality is, in those mind-numbing recordings with exes he pushes them every way he can to say how kind and wonderful he is, at worst how misunderstood he can be. But this aggressive, severe version of himself which he offers on stage, the no-nonsense explicit playboy who appears in his comedy, needs to exist to confirm his view of women as knowingly desperate and stupid. More importantly, that we consented to his behaviour.

'Let me ask the room a question,' he goes on. 'I'm gonna ask a lady first. If you met a guy and he said you can't come to any of my comedy shows, you can't meet my friends, you can't follow me on Instagram, all we can do is drugs and sex, I'll come to your house whenever the fuck I feel like, you have to Uber me there, all we do is fuck and drugs, and I don't wanna know shit about you – is this a good deal? No, it's a shit deal. Sir' – he turns to a man in the audience – 'if there was a girl who said the same?' The man replies instantly, pleased with himself, to applause from the audience: 'You had me at drugs!' They are the lads high-fiving each other in the pub – 'You legend! Top shagger!' The guys in the office boasting about how accomplished they are at using women. Such a desirable thing to be seen as among men, they were even willing to lie about being it.

On stage the sexed-up nonchalant pimp was so far removed from the emasculated pitiful man we actually saw. Who pleaded with women to take care of him every way we could, who wouldn't survive without us. 'One time, there was this girl,' he says. 'She went out of town, she was stupid enough to give me keys to her house. I didn't like her, really. I was tolerating these women for free shit, like dinner, Uber rides, you know, the keys to someone's house. She was out of town and she had a pretty nice apartment. I wanna throw a party but I don't want to do it at my place because then I have to clean up. So I do this party at hers. Also, don't feel bad for her' – he stops to tell the audience – 'she's an asshole. Let's get this out of the way, you don't know this woman, so don't be like, "Oh, I feel bad for this lady!" She was a terrible person, okay? She lied to get into America. I should have reported her ass to the fucking people, but I'm not petty. Plus, I need this apartment for this drug party I'm gonna throw at her house.' It trails off into a baffling story about taking a shit in her kitchen sink and leaving it there for her.

I know that party never happened. I know because the woman he was talking about is me. He was consumed by the idea I had illegally married someone to be in the United States, which was entirely untrue, but seems more a projection of his own circumstances having done a runner to the UK and arranged a quick wedding at the end of 2017. Nonetheless, on the few occasions he messaged me over the years, even as late as the end of 2021 (by which point I was in London, my birthplace), he was still threatening to call US Immigration and Customs Enforcement on me. In fact, it seemed he had even tried to get information through the Freedom of Information Act on my immigration status to have me deported from America. The wishful thinking of defecating in my kitchen sink would have, however, been a funnier joke had he said he'd done a shit in my Turkish fruit bowl which he'd ludicrously nicked. Either way, the contempt for me, in what was otherwise a fabricated story, was palpable.

Later on in the same show, he goes on to talk about R. Kelly. He blames the victims' parents but can't bring himself to say a bad word about Kelly himself. 'He's still wrong for grooming and doing . . .' – *he* doesn't finish the sentence, already bored by the thought of having to condemn Kelly – '. . . to be honest with you, I don't care. That's a question no one asks. Did he do it, did he not do it? No one asks, "Do you give a fuck?" I don't give a fuck. You know why I don't give a fuck? It's not me.'

At a comedy night in London, that same year, he tells the crowd, 'Back in the day I used to be a ho. Well, I pimped myself for drugs and free Ubers to a bunch of women and now they're mad at me cos they fell for it, idiots.' Men in the audience are delighted at this, titillated by it. 'It's a true story,' *he* carries on. 'Of course I'm a womaniser. What other options did I have in life? Scientist? No. My options were to play women for drugs, and Ubers, and sex. You can't complain, nobody wants to hear your big dick tears.' He fixes his stare on a man in the audience and says to him, 'You don't have a big penis, you have the curly hair of a Jew. They're not known for having a big penis. It's not racist. They're known for having the snip, though.' The antisemitism leads to more obsessive ramblings about condoms, then an announcement in favour of bestiality, clumsily bouncing into a few lines about Egyptians, Pakistanis and the British.

As with all of his sets, he is incoherent and his stories lead nowhere. Jokes start and punchlines never arrive. A stream of constant deflection. In every show there is excessive commentary about being a drunk or drug addict, which was something I had simply never seen, or got even the slightest sense of. Nor had the other women. He drank moderately with me, and I had never witnessed him take drugs, talk about them, or behave as though he was on them. While other women had seen him do drugs recreationally, again there had not been any sense of this being an ingrained or compulsive part of his life. It was bullshit, like a lot of things that came out of his mouth. But on stage he was now creating a public alibi for his behaviour, actions out of his own control. Likewise, his tales about being in gangs, being shot, a drug dealer, wild nights out, the parties – not one rang true. He has stolen so much from people – including their experiences, regurgitating them now in hyperbolical, aggrandised ways.

(I think back to Savile's words: 'I'm quite happy because I borrow everybody else. I borrow their joys, I borrow their sorrows.') Both on and offstage *he* had collated other people's stories to pass off as his own. Yet, a narcissist must still say something valid about themselves, and in every anecdote what was actually true to *him* was his own contempt. While I don't believe the stories are real, I do believe the thoughts and feelings conveyed alongside them are.

'The thing is, I'm having a daughter,' *he* tells the room to applause, which he cuts off with a kind of groan. 'I don't know how to keep dicks out of my daughter. As a man I've spent my whole life trying to fuck people's daughters, and I've been pretty successful. Most of the time it's been consensual.' There is raucous laughter. 'I'll fuck the shit out of your daughter. But I don't know how to keep the penises out of *my* daughter. I have no idea how to not make a ho. And my wife is like, "Maybe she'll take after me?" And I'm like, "You sucked my dick on the first date, and I almost sucked a dick for cocaine, so we're definitely getting a dick sucker." Weird about having a kid . . . So, here's the thing, I was in Las Vegas at a bar, and I take my drink and go to the bathroom and I sit my drink down on what I thought was a stool. It turned out it was a midget's butt. I don't know if you have midget friends, but midgets have real fat booties.' He continues for some time telling appalling jokes about dwarfism, before: 'We're flirting and she takes me back up to her tree, and we're making out, and I can't get an erection. And when I realised why I said it out loud and, much like most of what I've said tonight and in my life, I probably should have kept that shit to myself. I screamed, and threw her, and she fell. I said to her, "It's like holding my niece." I tell my friend, "I can't get hard, man, it's like holding a kid." He said, "There's a silver lining here. You can't fuck kids."' Again, huge laughter from men in the audience. 'I said I knew that. He said, "No, you knew you *wouldn't* fuck kids, but we didn't know your body was physically incapable of doing so. You just passed the paedophile test." I was like, I guess, I dunno . . . That's all. I just wanted to tell you guys a story. The truth is, I fucked the shit out of that midget. I didn't pass the test. It was incredible, it was like a hand job, but with a person.' There he leaves the stage to cheering and applause.

His comedy is a manifesto. Between the unbelievable fantastical scenarios, he was corroborating our own accounts of what he had done to us. Stealing money, exploiting women for cabs and food, breaking into our apartments, inviting people into them without our consent, the things he took from us and gave to other women, the booked flights he had persuaded women to pay for and didn't get on, the cheating, and the sexual assault.

Women are there to be used, our homes aren't safe, our livelihoods aren't safe, our bodies aren't. His hatred was for every woman. His exes, Muslim women, victims of abuse, Black women, white women, trans women, women with disabilities, his mother, his wife, his unborn daughter. He degrades them all on stage, and off it.

None of these are stage personas. Where he was a character was in our homes and in our lives. On stage he is bragging about all he has gotten away with. We were his punchline. The stage his confessional.

On stage, reliving his abuse, again and again and again and again.

V.

Like a good son,
  I learn to cook nothing.

Like a better daughter,
  I get arrested at eighteen.

That officer shoved my face
  into the pavement like romance.

My mother on her knees
  was not enough

to drop the sentence. God, can we live
  outlawed? I would rather

a dislodged fist than
  a purple cheek. Our bodies

bounce two beats off
  state rhythm. We move

authority like a strand
  of black hair. Enter him

from behind, just
  the way he likes it.

There are men who cuff
  the wrists of little girls.

There are little girls who hide sirens
  in the thick coils of their armpits.

— *Sanah Ahsan, Fugitive Arrangements*

I think back to those early days, my shoulders against the wall of a Chinatown bar under Manhattan bridge, the same bar he had taken many of us to on our dates. 'Your people are sandy,' he joked, 'but in America you're a white woman now.' I hadn't realised at the time that he had needed me to be a white woman. I saw this only when the dozens and dozens and dozens of women he had harmed stepped out. Our bodies varied, our heights, our nationalities, but complexion did not. Only two of us are not white. Both of us are white passing. I recall a line from his idol, the comedian Patrice O'Neal: 'You can catch a white bitch with some fruit and nuts in your hand. Black bitch you need to come with a stick. Black women are rough. White women are pleasant upfront.'

He too mimicked this sentiment on stage. In one recording of a live show, he targets two couples in the audience. They do not seem to know each other. One woman is Black, the other white. 'She's gonna be getting on him about shit,' he says about the Black woman. 'I don't have time for it. White girls – you don't yell at us. You know how many times she probably yelled at his face?' he says about the Black woman. 'Like, screamed at him? How many times have you cursed at him?' Awkwardly, she replies, 'Not a lot.' 'Not a lot?' he mocks. 'You see what I'm saying? *Why you like this bitch? Why she putting hearts on there? Why she putting hearts on there? Why she putting hearts on there?* That's her.' Then he turns his attention to the white woman: 'You'll say you don't understand, then you'll go talk to someone else about it instead of talking to him. And you hide it for years. And later, he'll still be cheating the whole time.' The set ends like this. Abruptly. Another revelation in the workings of his life.

It is not unusual for men to pit women against each other, to set us up in competition until we see ourselves as they do — commodified. It also works to keep us apart. Together we unravel the truths, but separated into categories we were the women who passed a man's test versus those who were proving to be a complication. It was easier for men to declare these women as the unreliable ones, the women who, with partial or full character annihilation, couldn't be trusted on anything, including our own experiences of these men.

Neither is it unusual for men to use race as part of their practice. White women have historically been venerated, paraded as the ideal standards of beauty and male preference. But *he* had taken the damaging tropes of Angry Black Woman and affable polite whiteness, then gone one step further in perpetuating them. Black women were too hostile to take his shit, so why bother with them? White women were easy to manipulate and use. Even historical racism worked its way into a formula for his abuse.

I think back to my conversation with Olivia; how he had described his kindness in the beginning as 'leaving nuts and berries' and how eerily close to Patrice O'Neal's stand-up this was. *He* was a man of no conscience, and what we know of racism, misogyny, homophobia and the like is that a lack of remorse, and self-service are a breeding ground for each of these. He identified with, and drew from, the worst aspects of society in order to survive not as part of a community, but as one singular self-satisfying individual.

White women (or those who appeared to be white) were his physical victims, but not without understanding his victimisation of Black women too, who he considered not to have anything worth taking from. There is more at play here than his impression recounted in his joke that Black women are too combative to fool – already a social construct used to position Blackness as unlovable. As well as this, for him – for many – comes the belief that there is no wealth in Blackness. No disposable income to benefit his scams, no perceived successes to ride on the coattails of. He rested on the bias that Black women have nothing to give. There's more: while personal gain has always been his modus operandi, this was still a man who lived in an America that understood status to be as momentous as money, and that whiteness – or one's proximity to it – was itself a prize. He had divided women by what he, and society, deemed our undesirable traits, and kept dividing.

For me, my religion and appearance did not, and will not, align. It was as though I had tricked him somehow, fooled him with the reality that faith, culture and ethnicity are nuanced. This was a man who lived in an America, New York no less, that coached its citizens in duality: 9/11 versus Islamic terrorism, Bush versus the Middle East, US Marines versus Bin Laden. In the world of binaries there was little public celebration in being with a woman who might be dropped into the latter of each grouping. 'Your people are sandy,' he had joked that first time. Then, another evening, when he professed that he had read the Qur'an and accused me of being a bad 'sand n****r' because I hadn't in full.

Two years later I am sent a recording of a podcast he has made with his wife. He has asked her to compile a list of the men she has slept with. 'Are those Muslim names?' His tone is one of ridicule. 'That's disgusting!' He laughs. 'You won't catch me with any Muslims.'

I turned it off.

I thought back to a date I had gone on in the Meatpacking District, with the friend of a friend. This man had moved to America some years before and these binaries had been clear to him all along, forced out of Baghdad as a refugee before living in Damascus, then Istanbul, finally settling in New York. His success in a Middle Eastern metal band had captured the attention of well-known magazines and, with it, the scrutiny of Islamic terror organisations. He spoke frankly about this during our first meeting, sat with friends in the darkly painted living room of his Ridgewood apartment. We drank beer and he drummed a doumbek that he held between his shalwar-covered knees, his roommate playing guitar and singing stunningly in

Arabic. They played us Ilham al-Madfai and Lena Chamamyan from their speakers, singing their own verses between the recordings. I felt at home, whatever this means, and on leaving that evening I stepped out into the sticky Brooklyn air as though I were a member of somewhere.

A few weeks passed between this night and our next meeting in Manhattan. We had spent no more than forty minutes together when he walked outside, waved his hand over his shoulder and said, 'Go home!' I did what anyone might do: I thought back quickly on the moments before this, inside the bar. His friend had served me a drink, then shared an anecdote about nothing of great relevance. I had done the same. There had been some laughter. A quick shot of tequila. Nothing struck me as obvious. I asked him why: 'You are just another bitch from Britain,' he shouted. 'You are like all these other NGO bitches I meet. I thought perhaps I had met someone from our part of the world who understood, but you are not one of us, and had you been you would not be crying right now.'

I took a cab I could not afford, asking the driver to drop me outside my local bar where I cried in the doorway to the man working security. 'I don't belong anywhere,' I told him. 'Go home,' he said. 'That's the problem,' I replied. 'Where is home?'

But existentialism is not a matter for midweek late nights outside your nearest dive bar, and so the man working the door hugged me, and I walked the short distance to my apartment that had not even been able to protect me.

What I had meant when I said 'I don't belong anywhere' is that I am not someone who can be loved. I am too Muslim, and not Muslim enough. I am too brown, and clearly not brown enough. I am too British, and not British enough. I am fine to look at, but not pretty enough. I am successful, but not successful enough. I am smart, and so not tranquil enough. I am vulnerable, and so not sane enough. I am not, I am not, I am not, I am not ever enough. I have understood my worth as a woman in terms of absence, in terms of everything I am not.

No one should love you, *his* message had read on the day of the clinic. But where there are men who do not love themselves, there can be no motivation for them to love you. It was never about you – remember this. I try to remember this. Because I have spent a lifetime feeling homeless. And let that be the response of a child of refugees, perhaps. An immigrant. An immigrant again. A woman.

Because hadn't we known all along that your home – whether your land or your body – can be taken from you in an instant.

Still, it takes more than one man to colonise a whole city.

★

In the weeks following the blow-up from the Instagram post, I thought even more about his friends.

I thought of the people he had presented to us, each talented and with their own successes. There were the photographers who took well-framed stills of brightly coloured street life; there were the designers and fashion editors; the people who ran their own successful businesses; the friends who were well travelled; then, those who were family people. He posed for photographs holding their babies. He walked in the noteworthy lives they had crafted, which he had curated himself within. He surrounded himself with worth. It was an alibi. They were props and, finally, they too had come to see this.

I had never met his friend Dante because he lived on the West Coast, but I had seen his photography online before. They had originally met through Alyse, who cut off contact with Dante and anyone else who stayed friends with *him* after her break-up.

'Every night he was out with a different girl,' Dante said, putting it down to the end of *his* relationship with with Alyse, a frivolous release after years in a serious commitment. Dante thought nothing of it. Even when the Instagram post first exploded, he paid no attention to it. Before Dante had a chance to read it properly, *he* had jumped the gun and messaged all of their friends with *his* own damage control. 'He said it was some girl who wanted to date him, and he didn't want her.' So Dante ignored it. 'There are some women who are like that – they become scorned,' Dante told me. 'As a male you think, I've been in a situation like that, I know people who've been in a situation like that. And I don't want to dig too deep in someone's trauma.'

I was used to hearing this. The idea that women exaggerate, become hysterical, and lie for the purpose of revenge. It's why, I suppose, so many rape victims are often not believed. There is always an alternative space where the only victims are men at the hands of a woman's contemptuous imagination.

I have seen it verified by other women too. I have been that woman. Willing to believe my partner when he says his ex is unstable, deluded, unreasonable, perhaps even a liar.

A woman I had known became pregnant by a man who angrily gave her little option but a swift abortion, then refused her any care at all. At the same time he began a relationship with someone new. As the woman dealt with her distress alone, the man's new girlfriend insisted to their shared friends that none of it had ever happened. In fact, it seemed the girlfriend had been much keener to spread this version than the man was. For the new girlfriend, the previous woman was an inconvenient reminder of who her boyfriend was, evidence that this man was just as capable of doing the same to her. And so she would sooner sink into a falsity that another woman had lied about being pregnant, lied about being heartlessly neglected, lied about being bullied, because if the ex was crazy, deceitful, the problem, bitter, it meant the new girlfriend was safe. But we are all someone's psycho ex-girlfriend, aren't we?

I think back to *his* friend who I had reached out to on the day of the clinic. I remember seeing his comment on the thread, and how (publicly) shocked he claimed to be. You knew, I replied to him openly, I told you that day what had happened to me. 'When you messaged me I was completely lost as to what was happening,' he wrote back. 'He told me you and him were having an affair and that he was just caught up in the love triangle between you and your husband.'

Again, how easy it was to believe the absurdity in such a lie, easier, somehow, to accept the plot worthy of a telenovela in which an unfaithful married woman concocts such a corrupt and extreme narrative for vengeance. They preferred this unhinged extreme over the common reality of cowardly abusive men who abandon responsibility when it suits them.

'I do not take this lightly' – this same friend wrote to us all openly on the thread. 'Playing with other people's lives like this is sick. No one deserves to go through this.'

They are since good friends again.

Eventually, even Dante was forced to take another look at the thread when he was alerted to it again by more friends, which authenticated it for him. 'When I read the comments properly, I was upset for multiple reasons,' Dante tells me. 'I was upset because of the whole thing with his mother having cancer. My mother passed away from cancer, and to know someone was out there telling fraudulent stories about that — it's no joke.' Had *he* ever mentioned having a sick mother to his friends before? I asked. 'No. He'd never said that to anyone. She's alive and well in Atlanta.'

I tell Dante what happened to me. I talk candidly about the abortion. Being coerced. Being left. Being robbed. 'To me the part that was upsetting is that he stole from people,' Dante says. 'Not just financially, but personal items that people worked for.'

I suppose this is where we differ. In the many weeks and months after, it was the loss of total bodily autonomy that haunted me almost daily. I felt the absence of a pregnancy, a baby, even — not the absence of my expensive wireless headphones, or bracelets, or clothes, and so on.

Still, I don't doubt the fall-out from the post was hard for many of *his* friends. But even within his social circles he had not always upheld his side of the illusion. In 2013, out in Los Angeles, he had convinced a group of friends that he was a qualified biochemist and knew how to brew liquid hallucinogens from his kitchen. Presenting his friends with homemade bottles, he insisted he had already consumed his own, although no one had seen him do it. One bottle, his friend Mike recalls, appeared to have the label removed and looked different from the others. This one, he had insisted, was for Mike.

Whatever was in that bottle put Mike in hospital. 'I had the general feeling he did that on purpose but I didn't know why. I couldn't push it with him because I had nothing other than a gut feeling. From there on I was always very watchful of my drinks around him. He would make a lot of jokes about drugging people, or sprinkling Plan B into women's drinks. We wrote it off as him trying out dark material for the stage, but it was always in the back of my mind.'

Mike moved to New York. Coincidentally they moved the same weekend, and it was this that brought them back into each other's social circles. Until then they had not seen much of each other since the incident with the liquid. By that point Mike had heard that *he* had been fired from his job in LA because he had cancer and took a sick day which the company hadn't approved, but Mike had also heard the rumours of grand larceny.

When I call Mike, he is sitting in his apartment and through conversation we realise we live a block apart. 'You've probably been to my parties.' I doubt it, I say, I rarely went anywhere with him because he said he had agoraphobia. Mike laughs. 'That's some shit I've never heard. He had a known history of lying. He would say some things that just seemed like he was lying for no reason. But it was well crafted, because it was just enough to question it but not prove it. The lies didn't seem malicious, they were just strange, or about whether he would show up somewhere and then he wouldn't.'

Mike was friendly. He gave thoughtful answers to the questions I asked and often hesitated when considering his own complicity. 'He was obsessed with Patrice O'Neal. And if you ever listen to Patrice it puts you in the mindset of what *he* thinks of women too. There was a disdain for them. *His* whole thing was that all men hate women, and all men deal with women so they can have sex.'

I think of one particular O'Neal line: 'Having women work with men is like having grizzly bears work with salmon dipped in honey.' We were there to be consumed.

'He sent us endless pictures of women he matched with on dating sites so he would look like a god among men. Sometimes he would joke about wanting to open a brothel. His whole being was about using women.'

I think back to who *he* had been with the women he was dating. A man who had never experienced sex without a condom. A man who was quick to say he was committed to you, even if you didn't want to be. He had, in fact, desexualised himself to us. He had emasculated himself so that we didn't suspect him.

But with his boys it had been an entirely different story. On many levels they all knew what he was doing to us, I say. 'We knew there were a lot of women. We guessed he was probably homeless and staying between women's houses. We talked about how he was bringing a different girl out every time and, honestly, we didn't bother to remember what she was called. We were looking at her thinking, "Nice to meet you but I'm not even gonna learn your name, you'll be gone by the next time.'"

Perhaps you understand what it is to belong to very little. Perhaps you know what it is to live your life as a statistic; maybe as a woman, or a brown person, or as an immigrant in a country that never much wanted you or your parents. You have learned that your character will be decided by newspaper headlines and jingoistic government rhetoric. You learn the importance of putting your own mark on this. Of reminding people that you are a Muslim woman who can recite J Hus lyrics in one breath. That you walk to garden centres when you are anxious to fill your shopping trolley with folding green leaves; golden pothos is your favourite – they are hard to kill. You show people that you are equal parts shy and stush. That you put your books in order of authors who might have been for drinks with each other, or seem as though they would like to. You have seen that to be a number is what put your father in a prisoner-of-war camp twice. You know that to be nameless, to be 'just another one of those . . .' gets a Black man shot by the police, or a person shanked for a hood up. I think on all the people whose faces were nameless, whose names were a number, and where in history books they fall.

*

I suppose what I had wanted was to come away from conversations with his friends and hear they had been duped as much as we had been. That they too had thought this was a man with autism and agoraphobia; who seldom dated; who had a home and a career; a dying mother. My sense of shame might have lessened if we – the women who had been deceived – weren't alone. That it wasn't our fault *because* we are women. That it didn't happen to us *because* we are women.

Instead, what I was learning was that many of the people in his life knew he was living between women, knew we thought we were in serious committed monogamous relationships, knew he thought so little of us as people. He had hidden in plain sight simply by existing in a society that had normalised so much of his behaviour.

Wasn't it odd *he* had a different woman every week? I ask. 'It wasn't strange. He was just being a man. I have a lot of friends who run a lot of different girls.'

I had heard this before, in my conversation with Dante, and elsewhere, in bars and offices, and TV shows, and online, in times that stood before *him*, and since. 'Hearing him have multiple women wasn't anything I could change,' Mike says. 'I was used to having those kinds of chats. I've been a part of them, especially when I was single, so now I'm numb to it. The culture around single men – he seemed within his rights. We thought he liked having sex with a lot of women and just saw no issue there.'

I tell him there is no issue there. Plenty of women enjoy the same. So long as everybody knows what the deal is. So long as the sexual partners, no matter how many there might be, are consensual, aren't a punchline to a long-standing joke. 'Of course,' he says. 'I think it's been really tough as men to have those conversations, and we find it easier to let men have a good time.'

Masculinity was something *he* understood fully; how it benefited him, and where it acted as a shield for his scams. Within the framework of masculinity, *he* routinely and comfortably acted out his psychopathy, and got away with it. His schemes, his abuse, his sexual coercions, the pleasure he derived from emotionally harming women, could all be easily camouflaged as something far more basic: as 'boys will be boys', as 'men just having a good time'.

★

On the day he had left me at the clinic, shortly after I'd received the text *No one should love you*, he sent another, reasoning away his culpability as he hadn't physically hurt me. The bar really is that low for women, and what I might expect to be grateful for. Nonetheless, his boundaries were never intuitive, they were simply what he had worked out society might let him get away with, or not. Physically attacking a woman wouldn't fly in the male circles he was mixing with.

And so it was there he would draw the line, unable to continue under the radar if he did so. It was then, in the eyes of other men, in the laws of masculinity, he might become an abuser. But to be a man who lied to women about loving them, who collected women sexually then discarded them when they got 'too much', replaced them with a new one – that was some shit men could brag about. This was fuckboys, and players, and locker-room talk; it was high-fives in the bar over a cold beer; it was 'running' girls, manly, virile, godly, a thing to envy, a thing to respect, well done, bro.

How easy it is to abuse women, then celebrate it by another name.

There is a moment in the conversation with Mike where I am no longer a writer interviewing a man. This happens when Mike tells me that he, and many other men in their friendship group, received photographs of our naked bodies as we slept.

I think about my body that was never really my body. I think about what it means to be interviewing a man who has seen me naked without either of us having consented. I wonder if he is thinking the same. If he has tried to match faceless limbs to nameless faces. I am thinking on this when Mike tells me about the recording they received. A recording where *he* ejaculates without protection inside a woman without her consent, as she becomes stressed and upset.

I know when I put down the phone that I will take a shower and cry under hot running water that cannot set me alight. That I will walk laps around my block until the older Puerto Rican woman who lives in my apartment building, with her bright red lipstick, the sides of her hair shaved, asks why I am not wearing a coat that is warm enough. She will insist I go inside so she may give me one of hers. I want to tell her that I have spent my life swathed in the clothes of women who have kept me alive. I want to tell her why it came to be that I forgot even the weather. That I walked away from my apartment with answers I had needed to bury under a tree on Lafayette. That by now I had learned this was a man who was whoever you wanted him to be. That his male friends needed him to act the part of player as much as he had needed to. That he was performing his masculinity to men who performed it back, if in no other way than by remaining silent.

I wanted to tell her that what I needed was to jump on a train and ride it to Manhattan, up to Harlem, through Washington Heights, into Yonkers, then to keep going until we're not at this place anymore. I wanted to walk to Mike's apartment, beside the bank he had said, and knock on his door. I wanted to ask him why removing himself from a group chat had been *enough* when the photographs of our naked bodies landed. I wanted to ask him why they hadn't confronted him about the recording. I wanted to tell my neighbour that I hadn't worn a warmer jacket because it didn't matter. It didn't matter that one woman told us about Bill Cosby, because some of us needed sixty before we believed it. It didn't matter that one woman spoke of harassment, because we needed millions of MeToo stories to hear it. It hadn't mattered when a woman left a party feeling important to her date, to *him*, when his friends needed five hundred comments on Instagram before she even deserved a name.

I wanted to ask his friends why they warned their partners and friends about him, yet never took one of us aside.

I wanted to ask them why they knew to cover their drinks in his presence but hadn't told us to do the same. I wanted to ask them why his behaviour only became shocking once they heard about the money he had taken from us. I want to ask them why his behaviour only became shocking once they heard about the money. I want to ask them why it wasn't shocking, why they had turned a blind eye, when it was our bodies. I want to ask them why it was tolerable, somehow, when it was our bodies. I want to ask them why our money is more important than our bodies. I want to ask them why our money is more important than our bodies. I want to tell them that my body is more important. I want to tell them that my body is more important. I want to tell them that my body, that was never really my body, is not America's, nor England's, not my baby's, nor my mother's, not my lover's, nor my religion's, nor my government's, that my body does not belong to a street, or a clinic, in Queens. I want to tell you that it is my body. I want to tell you that my body is important. I want to tell the woman in the next toilet cubicle that her body is important. I want to tell the woman in her bed, the woman at the bar, the woman praying in a mosque, the woman walking home, the woman on a date, the woman in a wheelchair, the woman in a church pew, the woman in hospital, the woman in prison, the woman outside a clinic in Queens – your body is of great importance.

I want to tell you that you will know by now a sisterhood is so-called because a family is raised alike. That our bodies have been lusted after, mocked and terrorised, as though we are one mass.

Your body is important. It is. My body is important. My body is important. My body is important. My body . . .

★

Spring 2019, I met a man in a bar in Crown Heights, where the ceiling rose high above the barstools and the drinks were strong and quick to come. We talked with a rare ease for strangers. I remember that we laughed and shared stories with a comfort and familiarity that had not made sense to me. Since the clinic, dating was something I had approached with vast caution, infrequency and terrified cynicism.

But I thought I could like this man, Jacob, and as the night progressed, as the patrons changed, came and went, or moved from barstools to the yard then back again, went outside to smoke a cigarette, ordered shots and cocktails in turquoise booths, I remembered how enjoyable it could all be.

He liked me, he eventually said, and hoped to see me again in the future. And I had felt consoled by his refreshing honesty, speaking frankly on how he hadn't always gotten it right but had learned the hard way that actions, or lack of, matter.

He had a friend, he said, who had harmed women and eventually been caught out. My date spoke to me of the effect this had on him, how when he had been faced with the horror of these stories it had made him think hard about his own role in it all. His friend, he said, had been outed on Instagram beneath a picture of his face, and the women, he said – well, the women just kept coming. One comment beneath another, all these women, hundreds and hundreds of comments, all describing what he had done to them.

I ordered a shot of tequila, the low hum of music from the speakers above, the turquoise booths and tall frosted windows that stretched towards the ceiling, the pretty orange drink on the counter that gradually changed colour as the ice melted. And I asked: 'So, how is *he* these days?'

★

Perhaps we try to solve the riddle by living out the answer:

In 2016 I was fairly new to New York, and was growing accustomed to the way the garbage smelled in the heat and the rats that chilled on the sidewalk. I wasn't too familiar with the kind of Manhattan bars where you dropped the name of someone who knew someone to get in.

I ordered a drink. *He* said, 'Turn around.' He laughed. I think I must have laughed too. His face partially veiled by the beard he kept in those early months. We hugged and I know how it happened – he said it felt like we already knew each other. Then he threw in the word 'forever'. It was this word. Forever meant I had already existed elsewhere – in a parallel place. In the absence of reality.

He walked me from the bar to the DJ booth where his friend, Jacob, played music that *he* danced to, some old songs, some classics, and others you might hear everywhere during the summer of 2016. *His* limbs were free, comfortable, certain in his body. His cigarettes, tucked into a T-shirt sleeve that he had rolled further up his arm. Like this he told me how startled he was by our connection, an attachment he hadn't felt in so long. It was the kind of New York summer where night-time humidity suffocated the space around you. And in a cab between the club and the bar under Manhattan Bridge in Chinatown, his friend Jacob sat behind me and spoke only to the other men in the car.

A few weeks later, in a bar in the Lower East Side, I sat at a row of stools at the bar with *him* and this same friend. One man either side of me. Like a row of ducks hanging on a wall, one in front of the other, wings spread as if in the freedom of flight, yet nailed to the wall.

The friend, Jacob, carefully picked at a plate of nachos. He never engaged. If I am honest this was the first time I had felt unsettled. *He* had sat with his hand on my knee, smiling as he spoke of our future, and Jacob his friend – his friend just stared ahead, eating, as though to keep himself from saying a word. For the first time I had thought to myself that something fundamentally wasn't right. And I had wanted Jacob to speak to me. I didn't know why I wanted him to speak to me. I didn't know why he wouldn't.

When the Instagram post took its final exposing form, I read through the comments from *his* friends. Some addressed us publicly with a careful and distanced tone. Others apologised more sincerely for not knowing sooner. For not being able to act. Each of them, publicly, informed us that they would have nothing to do with *him* again. Some of them, it was clear even then, were lying. Others seemed equally upset.

I waited for *his* friend – Jacob, the DJ, the man who had no inclination to speak to me on those stifling New York summer nights, who was more interested in his nachos than in engaging with his friend's new love – to comment on the post. I refreshed the post again and again and I waited for it. I had wanted to hear this man finally say something, anything at all.

★

It is his silence that I finally recognise. In 2019, when Crown Heights' bars with turquoise booths and drinks with brightly coloured straws are replaced by speechlessness. Like this I remembered him.

Slowly, Jacob asked, 'How do you know him?'

How do you think? I said.

'That was you,' he said. 'Your comment on the post. I remember which one was yours.'

Do you remember me beyond that? I asked. Meeting me. That first night in the club, in the cab, on the road beneath Manhattan Bridge in Chinatown, in the bar on the Lower East Side – do you remember now, on that evening three years earlier, sat beside me, just like this, where you hadn't said a word?

'I'm sorry,' he said.

For which part? I asked. For enabling *him*? For meeting a different woman every night, then thinking nothing of it? For turning a blind eye to *his* treatment and opinions of women, until the post, until you heard about what *he* had done with our money, and not what you knew then to be our disposable bodies? For not remembering me? For not speaking to me on those nights like I am an actual person?

132

My invisibility came from belonging to a mass of conquests. I was not an individual.

Jacob had not spoken to me on those nights because he had known I would not be there for the following one; that there would be another woman instead, and another, and another, until we were a tangle of comments beneath an illustration of his friend's face.

I considered this: had I needed to be someone this man was attracted to first, before I was finally worth talking to?

★

In those first days of the Instagram post erupting, the women created a group chat and consoled each other within it, a chain of advice and strength in numbers, watching as the content grew stranger and more overwhelming. At the same time *his* friends had done this too. They followed the thread together in their own group chat, comforting each other through the mayhem. Both sides of the same story. *His* friend, Jacob, the man I was now drinking beside, who I had been enjoying an evening with on a warm spring night, had not spoken to *him* since that day. Still, he was ashamed, and remained shaken by it. Those endless comments had shocked him − what *he* had done had shocked Jacob, and so did his own thoughtless complicity.

He was still haunted by it some days. We all were. Three years later, in a bar in Crown Heights, on realising who Jacob was, I hadn't wanted him to leave right away. He too had originally thought to stand up and go, run for the hills, he said, but the pull was too strong, and he couldn't. We now wanted to sit together for as long as we could – as though the two of us no longer side by side would disarrange the riddle again.

Time had collided. As though we already knew each other. 'Forever'. It was this word. Forever meant we had all already existed elsewhere – in a parallel place. In the absence of reality.

And the bar closed. And the lights came on. And the bartenders cleared empty glasses from around us, still sitting, like wall-hanging ducks, wings spread, in flight yet nailed to the wall, by now settled in the moments of silence.

vi.

Then we took the child with hair like
    the milkman out. Wrapped in the
    blanket and wet with soft bones dead
Buried with feathers of crows, a poppy
    like red flows,
bloodied the muddied moss of the
    pebbled brook stream.

Then we took the child with hair like
    the milkman
our knotted stained petticoats and
    bloodied dress skirts
washed our shame in naked silence, dirty
    shadowed with tears
and the milkman knew nothing and so
    never to tell.

— *Salena Godden, 'Milk Thistle and Juniper'*

I think about the advertisements for pregnancy tests: a woman holds a sleek white plastic strip in her hand. It is two lines, or a circle, or blue. She embraces her partner. She phones her family. Her friends cheer. Had I been in an advert for a pregnancy test it may have shown a person who didn't know how to believe the result. Who wrapped the test in toilet paper and shoved it inside her handbag. Who went straight to a bar. Showed a friend. Asked the friend if there could be any mistake. Sat with her head resting against the cold glass of wine in front of her.

Had I wanted a child, and planned for one, as the women in the adverts had — whose husbands and boyfriends anticipate eagerly from the edge of a bed or bathtub — I might not have wedged the result between my wallet and make-up bag as though concealing a secret.

Where are all the other adverts? The ones of negative pregnancy tests left publicly on bathroom counters? Of women rejoicing, relieved after learning there is no pregnancy, hitting a nightclub, knocking back shots to celebrate? Or — even more radically — a woman at a kitchen table staring straight ahead, the women around her busily laying the table, a lasagne from the oven, an opened bottle of wine, cups of tea offered, stirred, spilt, a positive pregnancy test for an unwanted pregnancy. But, thank God, they say, the anxiety and uncertainty of not knowing now gone, a useful result so she can now make steps to continue with her life. *This* is the advert I want to see.

What is the percentage of pregnancy tests bought by women who hope to find they are not? Why are their narratives always erased?

The first pregnancy test I took was in my mid-twenties in the Houses of Parliament. I am still bemused by that. Negative. In the bin. Followed by a few drinks beside drunk MPs. The second was in 2016. And moments later *he* revealed his mother's illness. The test was in my handbag, I told him, and *he* weaved into the conversation, with absolute precision, that his mother was dying – cancer, and it was ovarian.

Things that are not true include fantasies. That I might soon become a mother belonged to the same delirium where *his* own mother was also destroyed by her reproductive organs. Then, of course, according to him, she had died the night I now felt he had somewhat killed me on stage, only a few days before the clinic. As women our bodies were designed to fail us, to turn in on themselves simply for existing.

There was, for a length of time, a version of me who existed only in a relationship with this man. Who took on the narrative of agoraphobia and autism that was performed in a way I had no actual reason to believe. Who accepted his rendition of depression and cancerous dying mothers. As a woman I had learned to suspend my disbelief. I had learned to trust men by excusing them, learned to assume the best of men by accepting their untruths, learned to maintain a place in their lives by approving their shortfalls.

The truth is, he had grown more erratic in the days before the clinic. He told stories of a beautiful woman he knew who wanted to kill her beautiful child. He spoke of an old friend who had murdered one of his daughters, then killed himself. The remaining daughter, he said, also committed suicide. On the morning of the clinic, he arrived at my apartment late as there had been a delay on the subway, he said. A woman pushing a buggy slipped on the melting snow and fell in front of the train. Neither mother nor child survived.

Children died. More importantly, the message was that parents kill their children. And it was madness that drove them to it, whether mine or his.

For a long time I believed I had killed my child. I thought of the men and women who stood outside clinics like the one I had been to, holding signs that read 'Murderer!' I thought this is what they must have meant. I believed I must have been who they were speaking about.

In the days immediately after the clinic he posted incessantly excerpts from his favourite comics on his social media. In all of them women were dead, or dying. In one, Thanos stands in front of his hyper-sexualised mother, toned and in a bikini, restrained at her neck, chest and legs. Thanos has one hand on her stomach, the other raised above his head holding a large blade. 'I'm sorry, Mother,' the word-balloon reads, 'but the key to who I am . . . is somewhere inside you. And once I've found it and cut it out of you . . . I won't have to be a monster anymore.'

I see all of this now as a warning. If our bodies didn't kill us, if our children didn't, something, or someone else would.

★

I am reminded of a woman whose friend confided in her that he had three ex-girlfriends who all had abortions with him. This had been upsetting and unforgettable, he said. He would have been happy with any or all of those children, he told her. Then he listened to this woman speak of her own painful experience of it.

Some months later she became pregnant by him. He had been delighted, excited, told her if there was anyone he could have wound up in an unplanned situation like this with, he was lucky it was her. 'I should have worn my "I'm The Daddy" T-shirt!' he said, then went to the pub to celebrate with his friends. She stopped drinking, stopped smoking, she made doctors' appointments, all at his request, they talked living arrangements, spoke baby names into the world.

Then, as the days changed, so did he. What would happen when he had a new girlfriend, he snapped, and the new hypothetical woman would be more important than the real pregnant woman, his friend, sitting in front of him. What would happen when he was having sex with other women and she got resentful, now left holding the baby. He asked her to reconsider. Heartbroken, she told him she understood, was aware how important a traditional family was to him, that he deserved one, and she would terminate the pregnancy. 'I know how hard this must be for you,' he told her. 'I will support you in whatever way you need.'

He didn't. Instead, she spent the weeks leading up to the clinic alone. She went to the clinic alone. She cried later that night at home alone too. When the procedure hadn't worked and she went to hospital, bleeding heavily, then returning to the clinic, a mutual friend rang him pleading with him to call her. 'Why?' he asked the friend. 'What's it got to do with me?'

Two days after the abortion he posted a photograph of himself on a night out. Baseball cap and sunglasses, body turned to the camera, a friend licking and pointing to the words across his T-shirt which read – 'I'm The Daddy'.

Three weeks later he was in a relationship with a woman in their friendship circle, who blocked her on social media as though she had been the one to do something wrong. The pregnancy was an inconvenience, and it seemed now so was the abortion.

In the years that followed my own abortion I thought a lot about the anger men have towards us when we're pregnant, regardless of whether the pregnancy was planned or not, irrespective of whether the baby was kept, or wasn't.

How can I say this — a womb is a disruption to society. It provides children to a state that has no interest in offering economic, educational or medical assistance to them. It gives children to men who don't want to look after them. It causes abortions that are a burden to men who forego their responsibility to support the procedure. It causes abortions that are a nuisance to new girlfriends who are insecure about their boyfriend's intimate history with other women, or, worse, who would rather pretend their partners are good men and not, in fact, negligent gross abusers.

I am not determined by my womb. Some people think I am. *He* thought I am. It's why he targeted so many of us this way, reduced us to one interchangeable biological function to torture us with. It's also what anti-abortionists do. Bypass every singular or personal experience we have of this world — pregnant too young, pregnant by rape, pregnant too poor, pregnant when you don't want kids, pregnant when you have kids and can't cope with another, pregnant when you want to focus on a career, pregnant when your partner is dying, pregnant by someone you know will be a truly terrible person to co-parent with — and tell us none of that matters. Because taking away abortion rights has never been about the place of the foetus in society; it's about a woman knowing hers. Here, anti-abortionists, and men who strand you during an abortion they wanted you to have, are no different.

They all reduce womanhood to wombs, and, when they resent you, there is no clearer way for them to punish you than through the one thing they determine your existence by.

The past told us, again and again, that I had a body that had never truly been mine. In this instance my body belonged to a baby, to a clinic in Queens, to *him*, to his mother's imagined death, to history, and to the blood on my bathroom floor.

A week after my abortion I returned to the clinic. I remember very little of it. What I do recall is lying back in the chair as the doctor examined me. 'Good news!' she said. 'The procedure worked and you're healing fine.' I thought this strange. There was no good news.

The decision hurt. Physically and emotionally, it hurt. And, like the woman in the story above, I was alone and isolated and abandoned. *He* had not only used my body and my hormones against me, *he* had also put me in a system that kept me in a cycle of being shamed and re-traumatised by society over and over and over again. (Yet, surely I was not the burden to that system when I had only one abortion in the same year *he* had caused several.) The laws on abortion are frequently brought up in America – even more so since Roe v Wade, the decriminalisation of abortion, was overturned in June 2022 – and *he* had ensured we were in a system of continually declaring how fine abortions are, how easy they are, emotionally downplaying them so as to preserve having that choice at all.

'It's just some cells!' we say defiantly. 'It's not an actual life!' But in order to find the right decision for us, we must first picture what life would be like with that child in it. We have already fantasised an alternative world where that baby exists, in order to assess that it should not. Scarcely is it one or the other.

And so, women carry this trauma quietly, so as to protect other women from having the same laws that benefited us taken away from them, so that the reality of it won't be hijacked by abortion abolitionists.

But true and fulfilling abortion rights will start with the procedure, and continue with a space carved out for women to talk boldly, confidently, *brutally*, about the contradictions that come from having complete ownership of our bodies.

Fuck it. I will say it – I am glad to be childless, and regretful to have had an abortion. I viewed it as just some cells that scientifically cannot process pain, and also as a baby. I am allowed both. I *am* remorseful and confused and guilty. For me, it *was* a baby I still grieve years later. And enough times I have thought it was the *wrong* decision. But . . .

. . . I would have that abortion again.

And again. And again. I can't honestly prove to you that it wasn't the worst decision of my life. But you can't prove to me it wasn't the best. And I will take those kinds of odds, which come only by having a choice.

★

Soon after my abortion I allowed the doctor to insert a contraceptive implant inside my arm so I didn't have to think of myself as reproductive for a time.

I felt I could no longer be trusted. No longer relied on to make decisions without others' influence. I felt neutered, like cattle. I felt I needed to be. My emotional safety, my comfort, what the hormones did to me, were struck out in favour of ensuring I would not be a burden on either men or the system again. I was presented with a catalogue of ways to, frankly, restrain my body. The pill was no longer an option – I had been on it for too long in my twenties and thirties, which left me at higher risk of the cancerous side effects. I had watched friends endure lengthy anguish from having the coil inserted, the long months of heavy bleeding and pain. I chose what I might consider the best of a bad lot. The list had not felt like options. The inevitable mood swings, the way my body would change shape outside of my control, change in feeling, the lack of sex drive which would only reinforce the idea that men enjoyed sex and women got pregnant, or didn't.

Until this point I had bled heavily, forcefully, blood that had covered my walls on that first day, and for weeks after dried as large stains on the pyjamas I wore daily, and in public. The blood that had leaked mercilessly across my thighs each day, that cut through the maxi-pads that wrapped me like diapers.

On that first day of the abortion, I had pushed my face against the cool tiles of my bathroom floor and yowled. And the blood came, streaming like water, so much of it, out of me, across my bathroom floor, then, somehow, down the white bathroom walls. I remember being on my knees, cleaning. As though moments before a foetus hadn't just passed from me. I scrubbed the floors wildly. Violently wiping the walls, as if trying to erase much more.

The size of a raspberry, the size of a fingernail, the size of a cigarette butt, the size of a button, smaller, in size, than a shot of tequila, larger in size than a sip of wine, perhaps, smaller than the blood on my bathroom floor, bigger, so much bigger, than the blood on my bathroom walls. I washed them clean on my knees by way of an apology.

I haven't forgotten – the blood on my bathroom walls. As though I had killed myself, and washed away the evidence.

But with the contraceptive implant I was told my periods would eventually stop altogether. *Thank God*, I thought. I hadn't wanted to see my own blood again, nor be reminded of my body that was not really my body after all. I had washed the blood off my legs, thrown out my bloodstained bedsheets, and had stopped bleeding for some time, as the implant had promised. But, despite the implant, a remarkable thing happened on the anniversary of the clinic: the blood came. Thick and dark and soaking through my jeans, it came. It startled me at first. It seemed cruel. But what I came to realise was that my body remembered me. This was not a year earlier, no matter how much memory it consumed. It was a different day, and my body was still working, still processing, still cleansing.

Eighteen months after the clinic I had the contraceptive implant removed. The practitioner carefully put a plaster over the incision and told me, 'You can get pregnant as quickly as tonight.'

I walked from the clinic in Downtown Brooklyn, through Fort Greene and into Bed-Stuy. By Fulton Street I began to cry. Halfway down Dekalb I felt the blood on my thighs again.

Eighteen months earlier I had been glad to no longer be faced with the sight of my own menstrual blood. But I began to consider that there had been something very wrong about the swiftness with which I was told – not asked – to go on a form of contraception after my abortion, knocked up and spayed because I couldn't be counted on to take care of my own body anymore.

The implant may have stopped the bleeding, but my moods shifted. I was depressed in a different way, numb even at times. I gained weight, I got headaches, and my skin periodically got worse before getting better again. My body, that was never really my body. I struggled in particular with the way I had changed shape. My hips widened significantly, as though preparing to give birth, or as though I just had done.

I could no longer recognise myself. When I looked at my body it was different because I was different. Everything I hated about my body's new shape was directly linked to everything he had done. It grew hard to see *myself* in the mirror, and not see someone who was made, pieced together part by part, entirely from abuse and trauma.

I had done a photoshoot with a dear friend to celebrate the book we had just worked on together, and when I saw on my phone the photograph of us for the first time I broke down, panicked, on the subway.

'I know you look at yourself and see the toll New York has taken on you,' he wrote to me. 'I know you look at photos of you and see what toxic men have taken from you.'

He was right. Where the tops of my arms looked wider, where my stomach rolled, and my thighs stretched, I saw a body that should have had a baby but didn't. I saw a body that, because of a form of contraception I hadn't particularly wanted, believed it was still pregnant. A body that had either stopped eating for weeks on end, or gorged itself, periodically. A body that drank itself often senseless. No wonder I hated my body. It had gone through so much.

What I no longer saw were my tattoos, each one carved up my arms as a tribute to something, or someone, in my life. The symbols of things that mattered to me, in a life that mattered. I no longer saw the striking grey hair I had inherited from my baba. Or my eyes. Or my nails. Or the bump in my nose. Instead, I felt old. As though somehow *he* had aged me beyond this world. What I saw was a woman with blood on her legs, who stood in the shower and hoped the water would be enough to take it all away. And when it didn't, let it dry on her thin pyjamas, and walked to the grocery store this way for all to see, admitting defeat.

Immediately after the implant was removed, I lay in bed and did little else, for days, and for weeks. I let the blood stain my mattress again, ruin it as it soaked through beyond repair. I played it over in my mind, obsessively, the memory of those early days. I could think of nothing else. For hours, endlessly, *endlessly*, I relived the memory of cleaning the blood, scrubbing at it as obsessively as my thoughts were. And so the blood, I believed, was sending me insane. It was the thing that had sent me insane moments after the abortion, and was coming for me once again a year and a half later.

I wished I would get pregnant again. Not to keep the child this time, but to have an abortion the 'right' way. To go to a clinic with a man who stayed. To leave with him, and lie on my bathroom floor, bleeding, in pain, with a man who took care of me and grieved the loss together.

The magical thinking. As we go over and over and over every moment that went wrong, obsessively replaying the evidence in our minds, again and again. Playing over the fantasy of how things might have turned out so differently. Searching for the portal to slip to a time where things turned out a different way, a better way.

I was desperate, *desperate*, for a man to care as much as I did about who that child could have been. I have never resolved what it means to cope with grieving the loss alone. Did it matter? Should it have mattered to have shared it with a man, one way or the other? I still don't know the answer to that. What I do know is that there was, and always will be, a *particular* kind of absence.

I have always menstruated at the same time as the many women I know who bleed. This will, perhaps, not come as news to anyone. But what I had forgotten was that the part of my body I believed was disconnecting me the most, distancing me from my own reality – the blood – was in fact the thing that was historically connecting me to the *chain*. So, just as many of us had periods together, we also relived our pain together, and we healed together – and had we not already seen this at least once before with the MeToo movement, with every late-night kitchen-table conversation where women gathered, in WhatsApp groups where women turned to be listened to, or in public toilets where women who didn't know each other hugged a stranger by the sinks?

If women are harmonised by the moon, they are related by the blood they've lost together. And so women spoke against their abusers with each other's words, as ocean tides fell in sync.

I remember how freely *he* moved that night, the night we first met. His arms flexed at a different pace to his legs that seemed to know every beat of the music that played. In the months that followed he stepped lightly around my apartment, across my Turkish rugs, down the long corridor. He didn't remind me of the men who pushed out their chests when they walked a rougher neighbourhood. Nor the boys who dragged their heels. His was a kind of effortless sail that belongs to a person who believes themselves to be safe.

Months later I remember the jealousy I felt towards how easily he connected with his own body. That winter I was paralysed by mine. The food I could no longer eat, the smells that overcame me, the hand – my hand – that reached to shield my stomach in busy places.

In the early weeks of my pregnancy – when the thought of ever becoming this way seemed impossible somehow – my oldest friend came to New York. We shared a bed in my Brooklyn apartment, ate one-dollar pizza slices, walked the winter markets in the city. She was three months pregnant. She grew tired early in the evenings and woke frequently throughout the night with a full bladder. I began to do the same. 'I've caught your pregnancy,' I joked.

I have known Leah since we were children. We had watched many friends over the years become pregnant, then mothers, but if I'm honest I always kept some distance from their experiences. It never particularly interested me. Yet: 'You started to ask what it was like to be pregnant when I was still in New York,' Leah later said. 'You made constant jokes about how you might be. I think you knew straight away, days in to being pregnant. So when you said sometime later that you actually were pregnant, it felt like you had already told me.'

When I speak to her, both then and now, I am transported to Finchley, the north London of our youth, of bus depots and old-man pubs, and the boys who sold ecstasy pills, mostly Mitsubishis in the car parks of the sticky-carpeted pubs we were too young to drink in but still did. A place where we spoke of being women long before we were.

In another time, long before this, Leah's mother and her mother's best friend had been pregnant at the same time. Her mother took the friend to have an abortion. A few months later her mother gave birth to Leah. 'It was like history was repeating itself,' Leah said. 'I never spoke to my mum's friend about it. I think it upset me because it made sense why she loved me like she did. Even though she didn't want the baby, I always knew I made her sad in a way my sister didn't, but it was a sadness she sort of loved.'

This has always stayed with me. Two pregnant women in an abortion clinic, knowing only one will have their baby. Even then, even during something so tangled, women looked after each other where men would not. It reminded me also of my grandmothers – how one would accompany the other during her abortions, when contraception had not been an option.

As Leah's mother and friend had, we too navigated pregnancy for a few weeks at the same time. We spoke of our bodies feeling the same, while knowing outcomes are not singular. I asked her if I could speak freely about the process of passing a foetus without upsetting her. She asked if she might still send scans of the baby without upsetting me. For the most part we were fine to be a part of the other's experience, and still set parameters.

That spring her daughter was born. I flew back to England. I jumped in a car with a friend and drove the two hours to see her and the baby. 'Cry,' the friend instructed, 'cry now – get it out of your system before we get there.' We arrived at a country pub. A live band played. The beers were cheap. We ate scampi and chips and watched the grey waves crash nearby. Leah talked openly about how stressful the birth had been and I remember checking in with her. She gave me her baby to hold, and our friend checked in with me. There is a space where women simply get it: where we share location settings before Hinge dates; photograph the licence plate of a cab before climbing into it; rifle through our handbags for a tampon, passing it to the stranger in the toilet cubicle next to ours. As women our experiences may always be different, but as she held her baby, the waves that crashed beside us still had a tide that remained in sync with the moon.

★

Motherhood is not binary: the women who want children, and the women who don't. There is a crossover that takes place on both sides, envy on both sides, doubt on both sides.

I have not given birth as we recognise. Nor do I know how it feels to love a child that is biologically mine. What I do know is that children are a contentious issue. There are the women who cannot have children, the women who have lost children, women who have miscarried or aborted, who, perhaps, have not told those closest to them, and the women who want children but may now be too old to have them, who are too sick to have them, the women who are too poor, who are not mentally healthy enough, or whose partners don't want kids, or whose partners are too sick to have kids, and so on and so on.

I also know there are the women who regret having children. Who look at their friends who don't have children and miss the extra money, the freedom to travel, the nights out, and sleep-ins. Just as I look at my friends and wonder if I would be less alone if I had a child, if it's the kind of responsibility I actually need, if I am missing love.

I am not a mother as we understand it. I may never be. But I believe now I was wrong to define myself as lacking, somehow, as not maternal, on the basis that I may never choose to start a family. (Have I not, after all, played mother to every partner I've had?) I have loved my friends' children; I have changed them; cleaned them; told them off; put them to bed; I have buried a godson; taught teenagers to cope a little easier using the written word.

In the days when I still walked into schools with a bag full of poetry books and a mind filled with written exercises, I saw what a voice, or lack thereof, did to young people. I wrote words on whiteboards and urged them to care. Poetry is boring, miss, they said, and some of the time I agreed with them. One girl, fifteen years old, had the kind of surliness I recognised in the girls I went to school with – those girls who slammed each other's faces into fire escapes, who grabbed hair over a cuss, or a kiss with another's boyfriend. This girl folded her arms. She stepped with an attitude. She walked out of class. Then came back and left her pen untouched in front of her. 'This is shit,' she told me, with all the unkind and brutal honesty a person still closer to childhood can possess. I was fed up. It doesn't have to be, I told her. It isn't shit to speak about whatever you want, however you want to. 'Sex, miss? Drugs?' Well, why not? She thought on this, took her pen, and wrote about wanting to feel better. She read it to the class. She was proud of herself. She ought to have been. And the boys in the back shouted about how she was a slag. And she walked out crying.

I found her sitting at a large table in an empty common area. She told me about her best friend who was in hospital suffering from complications due to an eating disorder. She told me she cut herself. She spoke of having sex with boys she didn't want to. I remember the headteacher coming to us. I remember his surprise: 'You've gotten more from her in one day than we have in four years!' Which is to say: in four years, I have never thought to fucking ask her straight up how she is.

I rode the train back and thought of those young boys who believed their right to her body, then mocked her for whatever she gave them, or didn't.

I taught one more class that spring. In King's Cross, a group of teenagers came from the local youth shelter, as keen as they were distracted. 'Gotta leave, miss,' one boy told me, 'some brer's asking for a fight and I gotta go have it.' Don't, I insisted. 'What you know of my life?' he asked, correctly. 'What you know about being a young man like this?' Nothing, I told him, tell me. I know he didn't have that fight. I don't doubt, however, he had others. I don't doubt that the same masculinity I had grown afraid of was as terrifying and destructive for him. As frightening and noxious for the boys in the class before this. I think of them all some days. Wonder who they have become.

These are not accolades. This is not an exercise in self-celebration. What I am telling you is that while I am not a *mother*, I am not childless.

On the days when it snows, when the white gathers on the garbage bags on the side of the road, when I feel suffocated, as though choking on it, I remind myself what this all means.

vii.

ducking my head under each wave on fire
island i try to think of other times ive felt this done
w/life & survived
frank o'hara died here everybody knows
alcoholics die everywhere all the time everybody
    knows
he was purple wherever his skin showed
    i never thought of myself as a useless drunk
        i never felt
so unspecial *through the white hospital gown*
in the daytime it feels
like it would be easy to die
to dip my head under
            just a second too long
                but in the dark death is real
    like an animal up close
                he was a quarter larger than usual
on the edge of sleep you could fall
straight into & thru it   & nobody wld know
    yr name there
naked in the atlantic at midnight cutting a path
    where the moon hits
the water i could swim a straight line out into
    forever & nobody
would stop me. would know my name.

    — *Sophie Robinson, 'fucking up on the rocks'*

I lived. But this is not a parable of survival.

I was lucky. Lucky he hadn't killed me. Lucky I had people around me who could keep me from drowning. There is no singular experience of womanhood and we create the *chain* to remind ourselves of this. We stand beside each other in such a way that we may say, *Tell me your story as a woman, and yours, and yours, and yours.* I do not know what it is to be a Jewish woman, a Black woman, or trans, or gay, or disabled, or a sex worker, or a mother, or a mechanic, or a kickboxer, or a prisoner, or a pilot, or a seamstress, or four husbands deep (yet). Where I fall in our flawed verses of womanhood is that I am unlucky in some ways and fortunate in others. What we share is history. What we share is the need to talk, to say we made it or we didn't. Survival isn't enough and it mustn't be.

That first spring after the clinic I had eaten dinner with friends and walked my route home. The sky was red and pink swirls, the colour of confectionery, and a crowd gathered around the community garden by the end of my block. The gate was heavily chained, and a dog had been locked inside. It started to rain. The forecast for the night predicted a storm. Some people bought dog food from the bodega next door. Someone else tried to jump the fence. One man went home and returned with big metal cutters. The short of it is the police arrived. We pleaded with them. She was scared and alone and pregnant, we said. The man with the metal cutters said he'd pay for the damage. I told them I planned to take her back with me for the night and to a no-kill shelter in the morning. Go home, they told us, it's none of your business. We walked in the same direction, defeated, neighbours all a few blocks apart. Someone said the old guys that liked to use the community garden had a working dog and she got knocked up. Pregnant – I wondered if he thought we didn't have a use anymore.

I spent more time in therapy. I would walk the short distance from my therapist's office to Brooklyn Heights Promenade just to look at the buildings beyond the water in the city. I imagined their lives over there. I was hungry for stories that weren't my own. In the sessions I talked at great length about time travel. That is to say, I was in the habit of becoming paralysed by memory. She asked where I ended up when it happened like this. I am standing outside the clinic screaming, I tell her. I am always standing outside the clinic screaming. She made suggestions: to feel the chair I am sitting on, to take in the smell of the room, or the voice of the person beside me. She was telling me how I might come back to life.

Some days I took the train to Manhattan for the view, so I might recall a world outside of the corner of Brooklyn I had dug myself into. I wanted the feeling of being invisible in Chinatown. I wanted to be a tourist in the West Village. I wanted to eat a hot dog from a truck in Midtown for five dollars as though I didn't know any better.

A man stands in the middle of an intersection and cars drive around him. He is immovable and doesn't seem to care. I thought, to be a true New Yorker meant to step out into a busy road in order to cross it. How nice, I thought, to do this and have faith you will reach the other side.

*

I know why I stayed with *him* when he told me he was suicidal. It was because I know what it's like to be forsaken when you are.

There are the men in this world who are too afraid to speak about their depression. And then there are the men who brandish it as a way to eliminate responsibility. To keep from having the difficult relationship conversations, to keep from committing, or be there for their kids, to excuse why they cheated on you, to excuse why they smashed up the TV, to pardon why they ignored your texts and calls for weeks, why they put their fist through the door, to exonerate their own fucking chaos. The Ernest Hemingways and Kanyes, the Sid Viciouses and John Lennons, the Johnny Cashes and Russell Brands.

There are the men in this world who are too afraid to speak about their depression. The men who suffer in silence, weighed down by the archaic view that men don't cry or break or ask for help. And then there is the mythology of depressed men. The romanticised narcissist who is too wild, too brilliant, too artistic, to be tamed by sanity. (May I recommend never shagging a man who reads Bukowski?) I am tired of these men. They take up space from the men who are too afraid to speak about their depression. They take up space from the women too exhausted to recognise their own.

I have given up so much of myself to look after people, to play parent and cleaner, publicist, therapist and forgiver, until I am none of those things to myself.

He knew that about me. Knew I couldn't walk away from someone with mental health problems, so as not to disappoint them in the same way I was so afraid of being disappointed. In fact, he knew that about all of us. Some of his 'girlfriends' were women who suffered from mental health issues, or had lost someone close to them from suicide. Typically a man they loved. Where I was scared of becoming unlovable for being crazy, he used a version of mental health as both a shield and a weapon. For him depression and suicide were tools that allowed him to further manipulate women into both staying with him, and paying for him. Thousands of dollars at a time for, as he claimed, hospital bills and medication – money needed to keep the man they loved alive.

Similarly, he appropriated autism and agoraphobia as an alibi for his scams, as a way of managing the time he was dividing between multiple women. The introduction of agoraphobia into his relationships was also a way to isolate many of the women. Often, we didn't have many, or any, friends who spent time with him, no one to tell us, 'Actually, this guy is bad for you.'

Sometimes when I think about *him* I wonder whether he had always been noticeably mean. The answer is probably yes. But just as you would tire of him, speak back to him, begin to say out loud the things you were starting to notice about him, his mental health became a character in the room. It was then he would send more articles and videos reminding you how to speak to, and deal with, a boyfriend with his adaptation of autism, agoraphobia, depression, suicidal ideations, and so the list went on. He was controlling our behaviour this way. Manipulating us through our not wanting to be discriminatory, insensitive or hurtful.

What he also understood of the narrative that surrounds mental health is the unfair equivalence between it and violent, harmful behaviour. Mental health was, we have so often been incorrectly told, the reason people did bad things. Sinister things happened and it was unavoidable sickness that was responsible, not the man. Or so they said. And with *his* being outed, there came from *him* too a sense of, 'Well, what did you expect?'

Still, for all the lies there had always been moments of truth. Under the pretence of autism, he had described himself as a man without empathy, who mimicked human behaviour and was aggrieved by the brilliance he possessed but others lacked. He had, all along, been describing himself to be a psychopath.

He learned about human interaction not only by mimicking those around him but through the movies he watched, which is perhaps why so much of what he said felt as though he were reciting the plot of a film. It's why the anecdotes he recounted were always high in drama, full of twists and turns, where everyone he loved died in violent and tragic ways, existing in constant chaos. For most of us the shows were there to be seen and enjoyed, then not thought much of again. But for him they were tips and pointers on how to be a person. You may watch a show and think nothing more of a woman being pushed in front of a train once your television is turned off. But for him it was a good reason to offer why he was running late on the New York subway.

In the weeks after the Instagram post, he deleted all his existing social media and replaced it with another Instagram account and blog that solely spoke of the misunderstandings around mental health. Had we, as a society, been more open-minded about mental illness, he argued, we would have understood why he behaved towards us in such a way. He was the victim, he claimed, of both mental illness and now our prejudice.

Alongside his misplaced musings on mental health, he posted screenshots to Instagram of his preferred text conversations after the revelations. In one, a friend tells him: 'My advice to you after listening to all your recent podcasts, you might just need to delete all your social media and start again as you are starting your new positive life. Get rid of all the negative energy or just block all the bitches bringing all the hate. That way you can live your life in peace. You have apologised and explained why you did what you did. If these salty bitches keep on talking shit that's on them.'

In another post he publishes an exchange with a woman. She writes to him: 'I saw that post where a lot of women have made comments about you . . . I couldn't help but notice some similarities in the stories and with me . . . I'd like you to clarify what I thought we shared at some point . . . No worries, I'm not mad, I just want to understand.' He replies to her: 'Hahaha yeah! It's interesting. I forgot all about it.' Strange, given he had dedicated an entire Instagram page to the topic. No matter. He continues: 'I did learn one thing, regardless of mental health issues, if you are a man, you're bad.' His reply to her persists, it is long, a tedious reminder of how much he was one to talk and talk until you had forgotten entirely what originally brought you there: 'I mean, I do hope by now these women have actually found some peace.' He follows with a lengthy quote from a female friend who is posturing on the meaning of forgiveness. He carries on: 'She laughed because she said she could see or tell they weren't mad or posting until I started to express my genuine joy and happiness without them being involved. They saw my woman and how I paraded her and that upset them.'

In the screenshots he has cut everything else she has said to him, her thoughts are not important, and he ends his message to her: 'You were different, actually a good way you know is because you didn't feel the need to comment. Or attack me. You realised I was fucked up badly and you removed yourself. You also actually tried to help me in real life. Not just berate me and attack me. You realised your own flaws and the flaws of many you knew.'

Whether he was using mental health to position himself as victim, or alluding to his mental illness as a future warning and threat to others, it was always the largest feature in his relationships with women.

Where there are people too afraid to speak of their depression, there are still those who romanticise pain. Those who speak of being broken or damaged with a poeticism and desirability. I wonder how many of these people have truly experienced the revolt-ingness of depression. Have lain in bedsheets that have gone months unwashed, who have felt a sense of achievement simply from showering once in ten days, who have urinated in a bottle in the corner of their bedroom, unable to muster enough energy for the bathroom. Who have contemplated their death over and over, wretched, unable to tell anyone, not for shame but with the belief they do not deserve to be heard asking to live. These people did not speak of being a tortured soul as though it was something charming, something captivating. They did not use *brokenness* as both a pick-up line, and later the defence for egocentrism, vanity, and the absence of responsibility and commitment. I have met many people who posture behind their interpretation of despair. The men who provocatively tell you they are tormented, who confuse chauvinism for seductive melancholic edginess. These were also the men who were first to tell a woman she was too difficult if she cried.

My depression came long before *him*. It lurked through my childhood and fused itself permanently in my teens. In my twenties it was the thing I ignored, told myself the crying and bleakness were a hangover, or a cold day, or the news. In my thirties, after *him*, my depression was all I had: how it had driven me into an abusive relationship, then how *he* had kept me in place with the illusion of his depression versus the ignored reality of mine, and finally how it had manifested into something more permanent.

My depression, as a woman, does not come with the glamour of messy, disorderly men living like rock stars, or intellectual poets too creatively genius to be bogged down by rational normality. Instead, I am a nuisance. I am crazy, unstable, unhinged, a screw loose, the woman in the attic, a loon, hysterical, selfish, attention-seeking, a bore, a chore, weak, unlovable.

It was easy to assign insanity to women. I have been crazy for showing anger towards men who have cheated on me, crazy for accusing liars of lying, crazy for talking back, crazy for raising my voice. I have been crazy for knowing more about a subject, crazy for saying no, crazy for wanting love, crazy for expecting commitment. I have been crazy for crying, crazy for being on my period. Crazy to ask for what I need. I have been crazy for stating my worth.

But the truth is, the only instability I have is quiet, rarely public, and harms only myself. My depression, both after and before him, is something I am fearful to even discuss with the men I am romantically interested in for fear of being called crazy all over again. I am hostage to it — the unavoidable way my brain works, appointed as one more reason on a growing list of why I am not enough.

He deserved all the patience and understanding in this world. But I, as he had reminded me in those first hours after the clinic, was unlovable, and always had been.

My depression isn't interesting. It doesn't make me tortured and mysterious or a rebel. It makes me tedious. Both to myself and others. It makes me detached; it makes me inactive and idle; it makes me dormant and fractured, and disbelieved; it makes me grieve; it makes me drink. In those early days after the clinic all I did was drink. There was a point where I knew Brooklyn only by the bars I'd wept in.

I drank for a long time after what *he* did. And then one day I couldn't do it anymore. An anthology on immigration which I had edited and written for had just been published. Months earlier I had been with my publishers in Midtown where I was handed a beautiful first edition of our book. I rode the train back to Brooklyn, stepping out of the subway in Bed-Stuy, the lights from cars, little red, white, yellow dots, indistinct in the rain, a hardback copy of the book in my handbag. And I felt so completely alone. I had, until then, imagined this moment would be a joyous one. Instead, there was just this overwhelming sadness. I *was* alone. If I am honest, it didn't seem fair. There was something peculiarly unjust about it. To have worked so hard, the exhaustion, the weight loss, the weight gain, the years of death threats and calls to rape me, the slurs and insults culminated – because every piece of writing I had done, including that story, and this one, was simply to prove I am human. I didn't want that book to exist, nor this, because it wasn't *fair* they even needed to. The oppressed are called upon to comment on our own oppression, because that is all anyone thinks we're good for. People search for gods among men. And I am neither profound, nor good enough to provide the answers others wanted from me. I was still full of my own questions. And here I was with this encyclopaedia for the disenfranchised in my bag, and it was a burden, and I felt a fraud. In that moment I just wanted to be some drunk with my own distinctive set of problems. Not responding to the difficulties of a world I had inherited the load of.

And then it happened, a phone call from a close friend, locked in his bathroom, hyperventilating, sobbing, having a panic attack. I walked the three blocks to his apartment and let myself in. The dog shit solidified by the front door. The fish tank almost empty of water. We used to take bets on which fish was going to die next. I think sometimes we were taking those bets on ourselves.

I got him out of there. Took him to a group of people he knew and left him among them, then slipped out before he could notice. I cried the three blocks back and stopped in a bar to have, I suppose, my last drink. My neighbour, the older striking Puerto Rican woman, her head shaved into an undercut, her bright lipstick, later said to me, 'Mija, who sends a message saying, "I'm going to finish my wine, then step out in front of a car"? Even suicidal you're still a writer.' We can laugh about it now, almost. But the reality is I was driven to hospital before I had the chance. I was left on a gurney in a cold corridor in a Manhattan emergency room, a watch nurse either end of me. I couldn't take a piss without one. It was four in the morning before the psychiatric doctor came to evaluate me, my clothes and belongings locked up elsewhere while I lay, still in the bright corridor. He made a quip about booze, something about going cold turkey and my being Turkish. If I wasn't suicidal before, I told him, that joke certainly did it. And then I asked suddenly, 'Am I crazy?'

'No,' he said. 'I think it's just pain.' And just like that it was 7 a.m., and I was out on the corner of a windy Manhattan street. Still wanting to be dead. Or drunk, with no idea how to get back to either.

The short of it is there was no support. Not from the system, nor, I felt, the people I had considered to be my family in Brooklyn. The reality is, my friends – the people I had unlocked from bathrooms as they hyperventilated, people I had chased down streets when they drank too much, their character now unrecognisable, the people I got cabs to at 1 a.m. as they cried about men or work – now thought I was either mad, or an inconvenience. I still don't know which is worse.

At least one of them even planned to have me sectioned. It was abrupt, a decision made neither with me, nor, I believe, for me. I was neither psychotic nor a danger to anyone. Instead, as with most people in that particular kind of pain, what I craved was gentleness, to be heard, to be held, to be helped, to be told *he* was wrong and that I *was* worthy of love. Instead: 'We don't have time to worry about you when we're at work, quite frankly,' one said. Another had even gone into the location settings on my phone, by now tracking my every move without my knowledge, reporting back to a group chat that had formed behind my back where they talked more freely about me, not to me. The judgement was discernible and cruel. The night I had been hospitalised, my boyfriend at the time, a man with his own distinct set of difficulties, drank and played dice in a bar. He went to karaoke and belted out rock songs. Friends who had once called in a panicked state, to whom I had rushed to be beside, now could not find even an hour for me after the hospitalisation.

So, I remembered exactly why I had spent the previous decade denying my depression. And I planned to pack a bag, to disappear from my apartment, before anyone or anything could come and take me from it without my agreement. Distress quickly turned to anger. And the rage I felt was historical.

I have always had a visceral fear of asylums. Not because I am someone with depression, but because I am a woman. In the mid-nineteenth century, to be a woman was to be a wife, a mother and obedient, and so, faced with a husband who did not agree with his wife's less than subservient and dutiful views or behaviour, she would be institutionalised. Behaving in contrast to what was expected of a woman was plenty to have her declared insane. Women could be admitted for masturbation, being political, thinking too much, not cleaning enough, jealousy or grief. Not long ago, women were written off as insane for having children without a husband, or for enjoying sex, or talking back, or simply as a way to make space for another woman. The treatments at mental asylums were no such thing. Instead, they are what caused the women to actually lose themselves, trapped, not listened to, discarded as a burden, deserted – and finally everyone could say, 'See! We told you she was fucking crazy!'

And so I was sat in another bar crying, eyeing up more traffic, when my mum messaged to say she knew something was wrong, she could feel it, she said, the fear tangible and intuitive. And I did something I had not done before. I asked for help. I think I'm going to die if I stay here, I told her. And by that night I was on a plane. I left the city. Abandoned it. Away from the people who thought I was the mad woman in the attic, attention-seeking, weak, just a drunk, unlovable. I abandoned the apartment *he* had robbed. The bathroom floor and mattress that had been covered in my blood after the clinic. I left it all. Stranded the Brooklyn I knew by the bars I had wept in.

*

It varies – how we drink, and why.

There are the times I drink, and dance through cutting strobe lights, then brightly lit kitchens where the sink is an ashtray. Those days are all right. When I drink, and take unfocused photos of wide-mouthed grins and once-perfect eyeliner now smeared from sweat and lacking entirely in definition. Or share lipstick with strangers in toilets, calling people I don't know 'babe'. I have given the best advice when drunk in pub toilets. I have learned the most meaningful secrets there too. There is more wisdom in a woman's toilet on a night out than anywhere else.

I drink, standing on a chair and bellowing during England penalties. And watch you steal a traffic cone, or shopping trolley, and sing loudly to songs I simply believe I know the words to. And I drink, and buy rounds I can't afford. So I'm not shy anymore, to be funnier, or think I am, to play better pool, or think I do. I drink, and chatter about exes' new partners over cheese and olives. I drink so I can take an insult, or worse, a compliment. And take my heels off when the skin on my little toe hardens, and I piss on the seat, and get touched up near the bar, and I drink, and get punched in the head walking home, and I drink, and vomit, not that night but the next day, and I drink through the pandemic, I drink, enough to know AA isn't for me, and I drink to cry, or sleep, or text you.

People turn away from drunk commotion, too taxing to be around, particularly when we believe the problem is no one's but their own. Why aren't they helping themselves? we question disapprovingly, when so often the answer is that no one has shown them how. Or, that they don't believe they deserve to get over it. It's not themselves, or the people around them, they mean to destroy – just the sadness.

People are afraid of a woman who drinks. Because they're afraid of a woman who grieves. It reminds them we had a right to live better than this. They resent it. They resent us, because any sign that a woman is unable to take care of herself is indicative that she's not in any position to take care of anyone else. People keep hold of a useful woman. But a depressed woman, a distressed woman, a mournful woman, an angry woman, a woman baying at the fucking moon, she exists only for herself.

People are scarcely to be seen when a woman is thinking only about herself. Husbands detach. Boyfriends leave. Families disown. Partners cheat. Friends discuss your pain in greater anatomical depth with every fucker in the room but you. Listen, I have lost so many people I love to my depression. And yet, somehow, my depression is a part of what has taught me to love and care for others.

I drink. Sometimes to punish myself, sometimes because we've been punished enough. A depressed woman has no function. Apart from one – to warn you she needs back *everything* she gave everyone else.

viii.

you fall   miss your body entirely   land
   somewhere
in empty territory   behind the
   lines   your body   a foreign
   country   you cannot get a visa
   for   your skin
a parachute caught in tree branches   you
   awaken
in no man's land   gunfire from over the
   horizon   &
women   are crucified on hashtags across
   dark hills.

— Joelle Taylor, 'Round One, the body as
battleground'

Nothing changed. *He* moved to London and picked up from where he left off. Married a woman who turned a blind eye to what he was doing, and continued on the comedy circuit.

Male comedians in England were told about him, shown the Instagram thread from 2017, then continued to give him a place on their shows, which meant more access to women and a platform from which to vindicate himself.

He was surrounded by men who bought into and fetishised his absurd tales of being a hardcore American gang member with PTSD who had turned his life around and done good. There is a kind of rags-to-riches story that men are revered for. The street-smart business-savvy outlaw who applied his skills elsewhere for the better, reputation salvaged – versus the down-and-out whore who remains as such even with her career overhaul and catalogue of triumphs, or the successful women unable to shake off their troubled image. The Lindsay Lohans, Britney Spearses and Cardi Bs, whose lifetimes of achievement are eclipsed by a reputation as chaotic messy addict, or disturbed and crazed, or just some vulgar stripper.

It was the Robert Downey Jrs, Chris Browns and Mark Wahlbergs, whose serious crimes are exchanged for admiration, commendation and applause at how far they've since come.

Women didn't escape their pasts or backgrounds – we remained train wrecks, and baggage, and maligned. But a man – he got his life straight! Turned it around!

Made his mother proud! Changed his fortunes! Prepared him for the road ahead!

It was this framework *he* was playing to. The pretence he had come from a place of vicious destruction; now both righteous enough in himself to leave it, but still troubled by it enough that it explained away his difficult behaviour towards women, as well as his edginess as a comedian.

Comedy is an invisibility cloak for the men who hate women. It's not objectification, it's social commentary! It's not chauvinism, I'm in character! It's not a rape joke, it's intellectual critique! It's not bullying, it's risqué! It's not harassment, it's banter! It's not a slur, it's a play on words! 'Good' comedy is *meant* to push boundaries, *meant* to shock, *meant* to provoke. If you don't like it, maybe you're too sensitive, too literal, maybe you're just not smart enough to get it . . .

You can say whatever the fuck you want about women – and call it your job. If you position your degradation of women as your profession, it becomes possible to argue with anyone who confronts you that they simply don't understand your expertise. But tedious, uninspiring men who lack real talent have long been making up that they know best, redefining and renaming parameters to make way for their own inadequacies for millennia. And a lot of male comedians are no different. Comedians like this, and their fans, like to churn the line out that they're pushing boundaries, challenging

177

ideas, making waves. But laughing at women for being women? Putting us down? Describing all the ways you can abuse us and get away with it? That's not going against the status quo, that's going with it. That's not challenging fucking anything.

He wasn't getting booked for gigs because he was any good at what he did, or funny – he isn't. I've made more money reciting his shit jokes here than he ever will – he was getting booked because people agreed with him.

In a podcast with another male comedian, *he* says, 'If you ever see any piece of my comedy, I am literally saying a bunch of women I played in the past, and used all their money on me and shit, feel slighted in a way – they lost the lottery. The joke I made was I'm gorgeous and a man. I'm evil. I'm dumb. What other choice did I have but to use my beauty to get a way? I guess I'm like a woman.' The host of the podcast enjoys this comment in particular. Then *he* carries on, 'The crowd's laughing. Everyone's in agreement. I'm talking about this stuff on podcasts. I never hid it. I never shied away from it. You see how I talk about bitches? I don't even say *women*. People look at you and they go, "Okay, you smile and make me laugh, and you wear colourful T-shirts, so you must not be . . ." You put me in a box, when I'm literally telling you – don't put me in that box, cos I'm in this box over here. I'm in a box that I don't mind if you get out of pocket. I'm gonna hit your teeth down the back of your throat.'

And there it is. For once he's not lying.

It is entirely true that from a stage he was telling people who he is. There is nothing that I have quoted of his that wasn't already said to comedians he gigged with, to event bookers, to promoters, to his agent.

As the culture shifted just enough to shame men's public loathing of women, the men who just couldn't keep their mouths shut siphoned off into the comedy scene under the guise that this was now their work.

He tested his abuse out on stage in order to see which women laughed and were prone to being manipulated by him – and which men would let him get away with it. He didn't do this to us alone. He had a lot of fucking help from everyone around him.

★

In July 2018, seven months after the Instagram post reached its peak, a few months after *he* married a woman in the UK, Sarah met him on Tinder in London. He told her he was recently married but they had quickly separated. The reason, he claimed, was his wife had been seeing someone else at the start of their relationship and his trust was by now gone.

He had already introduced his mental health problems to Sarah on their first date, revealing that psychosis and schizophrenia ran in his family, but he was medicated and neither affected him.

As time went on, Sarah grew more and more suspicious of him, unable to believe a lot of what he said. 'I started looking online and realised he was very much still married and clearly not separated,' Sarah said. 'I realised they were leaving cute messages on each other's pages. The relationship he'd described to me was a world away from what seemed to be their reality. There were also recent photos of him wearing his wedding ring – he had never worn it when he'd been with me.' Alongside photographs of his very ongoing marriage, Sarah also found Zoe's 2016 Instagram post.

By the end of summer, now aware of the lies and abuse, Sarah confronted him. 'He had an answer for everything. He told me we could have something special. He wanted to keep seeing me, begging me not to end it. He told me the Instagram comments were by women who he had not been nice to and were bitter about his newfound happiness. Then he directed me to another Instagram account, which he had created, portraying himself as some kind of self-styled mental health guru.'

Sarah was irritated that he believed himself to be smarter than women, satisfied and smug in his own achievements. She confronted him again. 'This time he responded saying he had taken photos of me naked, sleeping, just to masturbate over. He texted a screenshot of a WhatsApp gallery full of photos and videos of me that I hadn't consented to, or even been aware of. I think he did it because he knew he wasn't going to get anything else out of me. I wasn't going to give him money or material goods, and I didn't want to be in this situation with him anymore. I think it was the only way he could demean me, to make himself feel powerful at that point.'

Sarah called the police. They sent three police officers to her flat and soon after she heard from the local Criminal Investigation Department. The crime, they told her, was the act of voyeurism, which is a sexual offence. The police asked Sarah to think carefully about whether she wanted to make a formal statement. Given the legal system's treatment of women, they warned her, it was likely to be a horrible experience if the case ever made it to court. Undeterred, Sarah wanted, at the very least, for his actions to be on police record somewhere.

As part of the investigation the police asked Sarah if she would let them download all content from her phone. She refused. 'I had shown them all the evidence I had. And I felt uncomfortable handing over control of the intimate details of my life to strangers. Especially given that I had gone to them having just been violated so seriously. They were never clear on what information they would use. Messages between me and other men I'd dated, perhaps? Would that be used against me?'

How familiar this attitude was: had the lady worn a skirt too short? Had the lady led him on? Had the lady sent naked photographs of herself to other men? Did the lady have many sexual partners? Was her cleavage on display in photographs on Instagram?

Did she contort her body to take a selfie that showed her pert butt? Was she promiscuous? A slut? A slag? Desperate? Bitter? Misogyny as a character witness.

'It took the police a really long time to find him,' Sarah said, but in February 2019 they had located him. 'He went to the police station voluntarily, not under arrest, and did not hand over his phone.'

He told the police Sarah knew he was taking the photographs of her, and because they had previously exchanged intimate photos with each other it was clear Sarah continued to be 'up for it'.

The police passed the case over to the Crown Prosecution Service who would take the decision on whether he would be charged. In March 2019 they decided no further action would be taken.

'The CPS cited my unwillingness to hand over my phone,' Sarah said. 'I had actually provided evidence, whereas he had simply said, "I didn't do it." They said we had both given "credible accounts". I took this to mean his account was therefore given more credibility than my own.'

*

Speaking with another comedian, *he* is talking, yet again, about some of what he did to us. 'This is what was broken down to me by. . .' he stammers for a while as he tries to decide who. Will it be a therapist? Perhaps his jack-of-all-trades aunt – abortion clinician and criminal investigator by day, flight attendant and Immigration Enforcer by night? Or maybe the Second, Third and Fourth Coming of his mother? In the end he settles on his lawyer and two detectives working his case after, he claims, he went to the cops himself.

He goes on to say the officers looked through their databases, including in America, and nowhere even under alias is his name listed; there is no record of him ever having been reported to the police. One detective, he explains, was even a woman to whom he gave seven years' worth of texts, all his messages: computer, iCloud, backups, old phones, memory cards, his hard drives. He insists she go through it all and let him know what he has done wrong: 'She said, "What happened here is – I hate to say they're scorned – but they're scorned."'

The policewoman, *he* claims, goes on to call us wounded animals. She is, *he* says, appalled women were sleeping with him so early on and expecting anything better. The blame is entirely on the women, the police officer is claimed to have told him, and the real problem here is how all of this has taken away from actual police work to deal with nonsense, where there's no crime, nor anything he should really be cancelled for.

Let me suspend my disbelief with him one last time. For old times' sake. Let me humour this meeting that bears no real-life resemblance to any encounter with law enforcement – even the truly terrible ones we've dealt with – and say, I agree with him.

I agree that the clapped-out neighbourhood piss artist showing up at a police station for personal vindication, insisting their officers read through four million five hundred and sixty-seven thousand, three hundred and five text messages about his mother dying just as many times, begging women for money like the pitiful non-achieving inadequate wasteman that he is, absolutely takes away from actual police time, losing actual police work to deal with *his* nonsense.

But, back in reality, I strongly suspect that the only way a police officer would look through any of his devices would be because he had been pulled in under suspicion, not at his own request. I know this because, unlike him, I've actually had conversations with police. Downloading the sheer amount of information he claims they went through would surely also have required corroboration with *us*, the potential victims' own sources. I don't believe any officer would make an assessment on his innocence in isolation. Nor would they so casually speak about potential victims, or his potential perpetrators, to him in the manner in which he describes, simply because if anything did come to prosecution it would undermine *his own* fucking evidence.

And yet – he's still able to convince some people that a police officer patted him on the back and said, 'No worries, sir. They all seem like bitches. Go live your best life.' Because while the story he told was just another typical lie for him, the attitude of the police towards women encapsulated in his tale was real.

As women the biggest perpetrators to us were not men, but our own decisions.

A long time ago, after a date with a man who had tried to drag me to the canal, where he could do what he wanted in private, the officer I reported him to said I should have thought better than to meet a man I didn't know well enough to begin with. The case was never followed up. Elsewhere, another woman shouldn't have had so much to drink. Another ought not to have been such a prick-tease. Another shouldn't have put so much of her body on display if she didn't want it to be touched. Another changed her mind the morning after wanting it the night before. Another craved the attention from accusing him. Another was merely after his money. Another just wanted to ruin his life.

Many of us – I'd argue most – don't consider the police an option. Either we've already blamed ourselves, or we know they will. Sexual assault had been decriminalised in all but name.

★

In the days after the Instagram post erupted, *he* shares a conversation with his wife. He speaks on and on at his usual insufferable rate. We were upset, he claimed, because we lived in a safe and privileged bubble where nothing bad had ever happened to us. We have egos that make us believe nothing bad ever should happen to us. This was simply not even close to the truth, from a man so disassociated from the realities of this world. Women have always shared safety tips along the *chain* to each other for this reason – wear a baseball cap with long hair tucked in; hold keys between your knuckles so you're prepared to fight back, ready a lit cigarette to stub out on a face or arm; take the brighter route home, the longer route home, the expensive cab you can't really afford then sit through that terrified too at the possibility the driver might be the one to rape or kill you. It was testament to how much we *were* expecting, how much we were waiting for something bad to happen to us, how much had *already* happened. The depressing inevitability of it all. There was no bubble, no safe space. We had already been through so much, too often. But for *him*, and many like him, safety was the reward you got for navigating the world faultlessly. It was earned, not given, and in the likely event something bad had ever happened, you only had yourself to blame.

He goes on to tell his wife that one thing he loves about her is that she takes accountability for leading men on, putting herself in positions with them, and all that happened to her as a result. This too was the framework from which Sarah's police officers were working – a position most of our police officers had started from – she got into bed with that man, she had already shared naked photos of herself, she was flirting with different men at once, how else did she expect to be treated? Women did stupid things, then blamed everyone else for it.

I had grown up hearing this. We all have. That women were not reporting rapes to the police, they were reporting regrets. The MeToo movement was just a fad, just a bunch of women who weren't strong enough to avoid the abuse, who weren't honest enough to admit it was their fault, who weren't interesting enough to stay away from the bandwagon, to gain column inches, status, attention, financially cash in on what was essentially all their own doing. The women who are seeking to be pardoned from their own mistakes.

In a conversation with his wife about the MeToo movement, only days after the Instagram post, he says, 'Because you're alive, doesn't mean you deserve to stay alive. It doesn't mean you should get fair and equal treatment.' Fairness, he says, is an ego-driven notion, and entitled. Who is to say a person shooting and killing others is wrong, he asks, simply because more people say they don't want to be shot or killed. In another of his baffling, tortuously convoluted ways he goes on to somehow parallel the Nazis with Muslims, and women who complained about rape. The best thing the MeToo movement could actually teach future generations, according to him, was to understand the world was not about what you want. He is at pains to make this clear. If you don't want to get raped, don't meet a rapist. If you don't want to get murdered, don't encounter a murderer. If you don't want people to abuse you, don't get introduced to someone who will.

We didn't want what he did to us, but he wanted to. We didn't want to be abused, yet we chose men who did. Why should our needs trump that of our abusers? As it turned out, our needs didn't. The MeToo movement only lasted a week, he mocks, because some women wanted to add their stories to feel special, because they wanted some 'likes' on the internet.

But now, he says, it was all done.

★

Elsewhere, another male comedian who is hosting *him* on a show, a man who has guffawed glee-fully throughout, says *his* victims and our believers constructed our narratives under a MeToo umbrella where no real crime had been committed. The women who spoke up had jumped on a bandwagon to cause shit, the men who believed us just wanted pussy. They are both tickled by this, in agreement throughout. The host says delightedly, 'I sat down and got me some popcorn! I was like, "Yooo! This is a series!"'

He cuts off the host excitedly, 'Finessed some bitches out of money for real. That's what you can't believe? They even gave the Tinder Swindler a fucking Netflix series.'

Women's pain as entertainment. Amusement. A spectacle. Get the popcorn ready. A podcast, a show on Netflix, a televised trial, a titillating tabloid article, a joke on a stage, a speech at the Oscars, for some – no doubt – even this story.

From Hollywood to home, from court TV to police stations, women's anguish was gossip to enjoy but not to remedy, tales to be told but not learn from.

Before the MeToo movement began so many didn't have the language for what had been happening to us, but now we were learning it so we could speak.

The moments we had written off as uncomfortable, as our own ineffectuality or mindlessness or drunkenness, had in fact been entirely exploitative. You did not have blackout sex with a mate because that's just what university was like, you had been molested. You had not given the persistent guy at the bar your number because you changed your mind, he had intimidated you. You did not stay with him after he slapped you because sometimes love is messy, he had manipulated you. He hadn't choked you during sex, gone straight for anal, grabbed your hair, spat on your face, pushed your head down on to his dick and kept going when he felt your neck strain without having the conversation first because it was the heat of the moment, he didn't want your consent. He didn't show up at your work after you broke up with him because you're his soulmate, he was stalking you. He didn't send you relentless messages and calls because he can't live without you, he was harassing you. Our feelings about all of this hadn't changed, only our language had. We wanted nothing from these men, except for them to stop.

★

Sarah and I stayed in touch, as many of the women before had. Then, in November 2021, exactly four years after the Instagram post had blown up, Sarah wrote to me. There was a young woman who had reached out to her, and was suicidal.

I tweeted my anger, my frustration, incensed at the culpability of the comedy scene that was progressing the career of this known abuser, the men around him, the order of things that kept *him* going.

New women saw my tweets. New women found the Instagram post. New women messaged me. They arrived in vast numbers. They shared their own stories.

I am sorry — we wrote to each other. I am sorry. I remembered the clinic. I am sorry.

And the voices came,
        and the *chain* kept going.

ix.

These days I wake up crying
holding myself in my arms
rocking myself like a mother
repeating
it's all right – i'm here.
And the room I wake up in
rocks in the arms that are rocking
me.

— Nuala Archer, 'Rocking'

I was by now living back in London. And women in neighbourhoods all around me had been through what the women all around us in Brooklyn had.

The act was the same. Meeting women on various dating apps. Meeting women in comedy clubs. Telling women he was ill, depressed, suicidal, relatives were sick and dying. He borrowed money and refused to pay it back. He got women pregnant and coerced most of them into abortions.

One woman refused his intimidation. Aside from the child he had with his wife, he now had another living in the next neighbourhood from him in London. While he didn't acknowledge the child, his mother did. Presumably the woman and his mother spoke over ouija board: 'Knock twice if you want to see your grandkid.'

Louise met *him* on Tinder in January 2020, while he was calling himself a variation of his name. He told her he had a child with a woman he barely knew in Germany and they had decided to stay friends and co-parent, the child spending three months at a time in either country.

They messaged for a long time before they met. 'He was really full-on. Texting me every day, wanting to know everything about my day.' Then finally, *he* invited her to a comedy gig he was doing as their first date. As Louise sat on the tube train on her way to meet him, a text came to say the gig had been cancelled and she shouldn't come. *I'll come to wherever you are* he insisted. Louise returned to a pub near hers where a friend was celebrating their birthday and texted him the location. The messages from her stayed undelivered for some time, until later when he began to text again, by now chaotic and maintaining he had been booked to do a different gig and was on his way there instead.

It took a few more weeks until they finally saw each other in person. Louise was flying back from an art exhibition she had been showing work at and he insisted he come to hers as soon as she returned, even suggesting he meet her at the airport. She agreed to meet on the grounds they had already been speaking for so long and there was a curious familiarity between them. He conveyed the same sentiment, telling her he talked about her in his stand-up before she got here, about how much he liked her, and claimed the audience were saying how cute that is and giving him tips. It was clear to her the impression he wanted to convey was of someone who was not just after sex, not a player looking to move on quickly. Even so, Louise found this strange that he was eagerly discussing her with a room full of strangers given they had not yet met, but: 'I'd come out of something a month or two before, where my self-esteem was low and the man made me feel like shit. And then I had a new person who was love-bombing me, giving me loads of attention.' They continued to see each other, always at her home, often during the day. He told her he worked for Comedy Central in New York and had transferred to London, where he was the writer for their pilots. There was no point googling him, he said, because pilot writers were never credited. The shoots, he told her, always had to be at night.

When he did come to hers he was always hours later than he said he'd be, the reasons long-drawn-out stories on why it took so long.

And then, a few weeks in, Louise remembers a day when he casually brought up, laughing, that he had actually ejaculated inside her – a week earlier, by now far too late for the morning-after pill. 'I felt confused. I liked him and it was hard to see it for what it was: someone who had done something sexual without your consent. I've been to counselling at a sexual assault charity in London and they very much consider this sexual assault. The police do not.'

Not long after Louise began to feel terrible cramps. She made an appointment with her doctor, not entirely expecting the results to show a pregnancy.

First, she called her best friend: 'And then I called *him*. He knew. He said, You're pregnant, aren't you?'

Louise carried on, 'During this time in his fantasy world he was directing a shoot in Soho, London. He went from saying to me, "It's okay, we can sort this out, I'm a feminist! Whatever you want to do I will support you!" to an hour later, when the messages changed. "I hope you don't, simply because it's not fair to the kid at all. But that's not a clear thing you can see at the moment, due to hormones and such.

Even the fact you think you're in a position to raise a kid now is all the more reason you should wait until your life is in a more stable position. Bringing someone into this world at this point is just selfish. Even considering it is. I don't think many would disagree."'

He told Louise that even the nature of their relationship confirmed it was a terrible idea. 'I asked what he meant by that and he said it was "just sex". I said to him I didn't consent to that. Everything else he'd built up between us — that's not what *just sex* looks like. I said if it was just sex why did he want us to write together, and plan all these other things together. His response was to call me lame.'

His messages, true to form, got nastier. Louise was by now on her way to Paris again for work, and he was insistent she didn't go, requesting she stay in London to have an immediate abortion. 'He told me I was going to Paris because I was only thinking about myself and my career. Yes! Of course I am!' she thought.

His aggression towards her was so horrifying, by now shocked by his behaviour, she blocked him for a period so she could make a decision on the pregnancy without the distraction of his incessant belligerence. Even so, Louise reflected on how co-parenting didn't seem an unreasonable option as, according to him, he was successfully achieving this elsewhere. Eventually they spoke again. Louise wanted a calm, thoughtful conversation away from the heightened, immediate, reactionary emotions that came before. Instead, 'He messaged me saying, "I don't care, I've already told you my stance so this doesn't concern me at all anymore. I have a load of other things to take care of including other children. Which I already can't. You went and let everyone else help you decide so let them help you in any other way."' The conversations never got better. The most he offered her was to meet again, not to talk about the baby, but 'because now is the perfect time to fuck. It's not like you can get pregnant again.'

'I made an appointment with the abortion clinic,' Louise says, 'and it was the same old story: he couldn't possibly come because he had to fly back to Atlanta last minute because his cousin who was involved in gang violence was dead!'

She of course went alone, where the doctor doing her mental health assessment told her she wasn't comfortable giving her abortion pills, unconvinced Louise actually wanted to go through with it. 'I was thirty-four years old and it was the first time I'd been pregnant. I thought, I don't know when this will ever happen again. And I don't think women should be ashamed to say that. Ageing – a part of that is in the decision process.'

It's not always the easiest conversation. Louise cries when she feels guilt at the thought of being pushed into a decision that would mean not having her daughter now. 'I felt so strongly about keeping her. But I was so conflicted because he really intimidated me and pushed me into thinking I didn't have a choice.'

Louise did what was right for her. She wrote to him to say she wanted the baby, she was keeping it. He replied, 'Never contact me again.'

★

Louise was five months pregnant when two of her closest friends invited her to dinner. They asked her to confirm *his* name and that he was a comedian. Then, her friend told her, 'He has a wife and child. Neither live in Germany. They are very much together.' His wife was in fact the colleague of someone they knew well, through conversation they had pieced together the overall link.

'I thought, *I'm such an idiot*,' Louise said. 'I'm having a baby with a married man. I felt like a failure.' In fact, Louise believed that he had moved back to America immediately, as he had told her he would. Only now she knew he had another family and they were actually living together down the road from her. 'Had I known who he was in the beginning,' Louise tells me, 'I probably would not have gone through with the pregnancy. If nothing else, I am forever grateful I was ignorant to it.'

★

Two weeks after I wrote about my experience on Twitter, Louise googled his name and found it attached to a tweet parallel to mine. She reached out to me, as many, many others did.

When the Twitter thread blew up his agent dropped him, comedy clubs cancelled his gigs, comedians publicly and personally distanced themselves from him. Before, it appeared nobody in the comedy world had taken our stories seriously – or cared. But now the people around him took swift action in a way I hadn't seen before. I don't doubt that some, likely much, of it was superficial. Men who are afraid their careers will end by association, men with no sincere reflection, guilt or atonement. There was no answer from *his* agent, for example, when I asked if he had watched *his* stand-up about abusing women and signed him regardless, or if he hadn't seen *his* stand-up at all and was simply just terrible at his job. Nevertheless, what was different this time was his friends and peers wanted to speak to me. What was different this time was how far my reach had extended in finding new women. What was different this time was how it all happened in only two days.

He made one attempt at retaliation. He posted screenshots of texts between himself and a female comedian to a Facebook comedy group. He was instantly removed, the posts immediately taken down. Then, after that, there was simply very little immediate response. No excessive Twitter reaction of his own. No frantic erratic justifications across all social media.

No new Instagram accounts invoking God. I didn't hear from him. No threats to deport me or, worse, the tedious paragraphs he would sometimes send insisting he was successful and doing well, caring so little for what we said about him. The places and audiences for him to relive what he had done to us notably lessened.

What struck me was how I had needed to become successful enough to do this. I had needed to have a reputable career to be heard. I had needed to build a large enough platform to be taken seriously. Even harder than this, I had needed to survive what he had done to me to achieve anything at all.

'Oh, sinner man, where you gonna run to?' – and when the new women came I stood in my living room, on the same rug I had years earlier curled up on, clutching my belly, 'The moon will be bleeding . . . stars, won't you hide me?' – and so I played the song, Sinner Man, loudly from my speakers, out over the alleyway behind my home, into Hackney, up to Leyton, through Walthamstow, with answers I had needed to bury under a tree in Finchley. Until we weren't at this place anymore – 'Oh, sinner man, where you gonna run to? All on that day'.

X.

I told a story about my shame
It got cold when the air touched it
Then it got hot, throbbed, wept,
    attracted fragments with which it
    eventually glittered
Till I couldn't stop looking at it

— *Emily Berry, 'The End'*

Time passes. It does. I was sitting outside a bar on an anniversary. Crying, barely. Inaudible, without action, watching the road – when a woman I had previously never seen joined my table, reaching an arm around me. 'We're all going through it,' she said.

'I'm grieving a baby,' I let out suddenly. 'I get it,' she told me. 'I'm having a drink with an ex. We were trying for one and had a lot of miscarriages. Seeing him today is going to fuck me up. I hope when I'm crying about it later, a woman comes over and hugs me.'

I tell her, *I'm sure she will.*

★

I am with two female friends in a tapas restaurant that has decent padrón peppers and an unnecessary variety of mezcal cocktails, when my friend sees a man who raped her.

He is on a date. I wonder if my friend will cry at the table, or ask immediately for the bill and for us to leave. Instead, she says, 'How do we get that woman away from him?'

When his date gets up to use the bathroom our other friend follows, loitering beside the sinks. She tells his date everything he did, advising her to get out of there.

On another occasion a barmaid in a pub I would frequent was on the toilet, door wide open, when I walked in. 'I'm fucking pregnant,' she said, holding up the stick. That evening she remained serving drinks on the side of the bar I was sitting, turning to me in quieter moments to release her anxiety, her fear. Around her, the other barmaid kept my wine glass full without charge.

Another time, I am waiting for friends in a crowded bar as a man hits on me relentlessly, unwilling to leave me alone. A woman I don't know walks over and grabs me, 'So great to see you! It's been so long!' – placing herself between the man and me until he goes away. When he does, I thank her and she returns to her friends, and I return to waiting for mine, safely.

Many years ago, one of my ex-husband's closest friends went shopping, and ran into the man whose house he had claimed to have stayed over at after getting drunk. She enquired how their night out had gone. Dumbstruck, the man admitted he hadn't seen my ex-husband in many years. She called me, right away, and told me. My ex-husband and I separated. The beginning of my life alone in New York. He cut her off for telling me. To this day, she is by far the best thing I kept in the divorce.

A close friend's husband changed when they had their child. She could detect his jealousy, the mother's attention now more focused on their daughter than the man. In those early days she didn't know how to go out alone with the baby. Her husband refused to help: 'Other mothers do it,' he told her, 'what's your problem?' As for these other mothers, it was them who took her out when she broke down. These other mothers, her neighbours, colleagues, who once hadn't known either, who showed her to navigate the pram on pavements, to fasten a child seat into a car, how to buy a coffee with a baby attached and walk through a park.

A friend's birthday, a 54-year-old woman with thick fake eyelashes and a toy-boy, takes me into the toilets and lifts up her dress. 'There!' she says, a half-smoked unlit cigarette dangling from her mouth, 'they took the flesh from my stomach and built the new boob after the tit cancer from it.' Do you want a fake nipple? I ask. 'Nah,' she says, 'I fed my kids with this one,' she points at her other breast, 'I don't need another one.'

It's the crying woman in the toilet we gather around for comfort and counselling; the woman half-cut on the pavement who we put in a cab, handing twenty quid of our own money to the driver, snapping the licence plate on our phone; it's wrapping your jumper around someone's waist when their period has bled through their clothes; the 'Text me when you get home!'; it's dividing up shampoo and shower gel in the gym; offering financial advice at work; introducing a woman in a new city or country to a trusted female friend we also know out there.

The question is: what wouldn't women share to help another? We share our friends, our homes, our make-up and clothes and shoes, the numbers of our therapists, our experiences with contraception, the sanitary towel at the bottom of our bag, our medical histories, recipes, and cabs, and the safest bus routes home — we share our stories.

On the day of the clinic a woman would leave work early. She would pick me up from my kitchen floor where I had been lying, gripping at all that was dead inside. The following day she would count tablets and prepare food I barely touched. There is fearlessness in the way women love each other. To be a woman was not newly discovered. There was no experience of the violence put upon our bodies that she did not already know.

Still, let it be known, when a woman carries a man on her shoulders, it is practice for when she must uphold her sisters.

★

The day after I met *him*, I met Maya.

I was ordering a drink at an events space in Williamsburg. A friend had organised an afternoon of music recitals by South Asian artists he knew. I showed up alone. I drank glasses of cheap white wine and hung out with the Arabs. A girl with an English accent moved to me and I stepped out of her way. I thought she wanted to get to the bar. Back then I knew very few people in Brooklyn and expected even fewer to know me.

She said my name. She had recognised my face from pictures beside my articles, and went on to say she liked my work. I bought her a drink. I don't usually do this, too awkward in myself to talk freely with strangers who know more about me than I do them. She didn't usually do this either. It wasn't particularly in her nature to approach people she didn't know. Perhaps it happened this way because we were both from London. Perhaps we appeared as lost as the other in a bustling dark room in the middle of the day. She had needed to get away from a guy hitting on her and it had made sense to come talk to me as an escape. As it turns out, I had needed to get away from a guy hitting on me too, and I welcomed her interruption. How often it is that women need to get away from men who are insisting on our attention. How often we turn to each other to escape them – more trusting sometimes of a woman we don't know than a man we already do.

I told her about my date the previous night. I felt lucky, charged and alive, and I had wanted everyone to know this. We exchanged numbers. We met for drinks as the weeks and months followed. I was grateful for her, Maya, no doubt because she was smart and thoughtful and spoke in ways I recognised. We sounded alike – this almost mattered in a city that swallowed your accent and voice most days.

Months later, and three days before the clinic, I stepped out at Broadway station and up on to the sidewalk.

The snow under the railway bridge was black. A few hours earlier I had heard about two childhood friends – sisters: one was pregnant and expecting her first child. The other, my family said, was just like me – happy to be alone. I didn't know what this meant. I still don't. But Maya was sat in a coffee shop a few metres away, and what I did know was how it felt to be powerless.

We talked at great length about a feeling I had that he wasn't going to show up at the clinic to support me. Had we, at that moment, been talking about him, or what we had seen of men as an institution? I don't know. But his continual absence, whatever his reasons had been until this point, was repeated and noted. We put it down to his depression, his agoraphobia, his mother who had been dying, and then had died the night before. Whatever the reason he might have given, we planned for something. My words were heated and agitated by history.

'At the time all of my concerns had been whether he would go with you.' When Maya says this, it is exactly a year to the day since the clinic. 'That morning I was ready to come with you. I knew I could clear my work schedule enough to do this. But you texted saying he got to your apartment just in time, and I relaxed because I thought, she's in safe hands. I couldn't have imagined what would happen.'

And when I phoned from outside the clinic? I asked: 'When I answered, there was no hello. You were just screaming. Only screams. Then eventually your first words were, "He left me." That's all you were saying – "He left me, he left me, he left me." I remember getting up, walking into a quiet meeting room. I asked you where you were. You kept repeating, "I don't know."'

I didn't know. I knew the road was quiet. I knew nearby there was a railway bridge. I knew I was carrying something inside me that was no longer alive. I knew there was a small bodega on a busy road a block away.

'Eventually you said you were in Queens. I looked up the clinic and gave you directions to get home. I remember telling you I was going to leave work immediately and come straight to your place. I got there only a few minutes after you.'

A year on, Maya and I were marking the strangest of anniversaries, reminiscing, the most unexpected of memories, and she recalled: 'You were crying when you called. Really crying. And I thought, "She's just had an abortion and she's devastated." But then I realised what you were saying. I realised what you meant by "he left". And when I got to your apartment you came downstairs to let me into the building. And when we walked into your home you just dropped to the floor.'

She had helped me to my feet, the prescription for the medication by now crumpled in my coat pocket. She walked me to the front door, but in the bathroom his toiletries had caught my eye. Grabbing them I had launched them across the room with a consuming rage.

A year on we laughed about it. What a ridiculous scene that must have been. Hunched over my bathtub pitching hair products across the place. Maya gathered them and, unsure what to do, walked to the pharmacy with me, still cradling his shampoo bottles in her arms. 'I carried them a whole block wondering what the fuck to do with them.' She laughed.

'We said all along that I was willing to go with you to the clinic. You gave him his way out. You told him before that if it was too much stress, I was planning to take you. Even then, I didn't understand why he would go to the clinic in the first place just to do that in the end. But you were the one who said, "Of course he came. He had to make sure I'd go through with it."' I remembered Jessica in a bar on Tompkins. I remembered her using these words a month after I had.

I hadn't known that he would do this – but I had *known*. Were you truly surprised? I asked. 'This was a pattern of behaviour. He was a man who was always absent. But all of his cruelty had always been in disguise. It always came with good excuses. But this is where he shifted. He couldn't get himself out of this one, so he turned malicious. There was nothing left. That day he tore down the illusion because you were catching up to him anyway. He went from being an unreliable wasteman, to me realising you had been in danger the whole time. You have to remember I met you at the very start of it. Who I met that day – you were a shell by the end.'

I could not make it okay. I could not make being pregnant okay. I had not been able to make his depression (if it had ever truly existed) okay. There had not been a lie that I could battle with. When I had dealt with one, another ten came. If it was money he needed, I didn't have it. If it was love, I had given it all.

'I remember when you had seen on social media that he was on the line-up for a comedy show in New York. But he had told you he was in Atlanta with his mum. I thought, "Shall I just call the place and confirm if he went or not – put her out of her misery?" But I didn't. Nobody wanted to say, "What if his mum isn't dying? What if he's not autistic or agoraphobic? What if there was never a suicide prevention clinic in Australia?" What kind of person doesn't want to believe those things about someone else?'

I think back to the careers of the ex-girlfriends we know about. There are two types: creative, or humanitarian. Those of us who are not writers, dancers, artists or in media are teachers, sexual healthcare professionals or work for charities. We were all compassionate and empathetic, perhaps to a fault. We related deeply with the suffering and care and growth of others, and he had known this about us.

'His language was very much about you and him being in it together. You were both going through *everything* together. It had never been about building you up. He kept telling you that you were both depressed, until you were depressed. He wanted you to be bound by tragic situations.'

The fantasy he had created was hard to unravel fully. In fact, I stayed somewhere within it until I met Jessica. 'It was classic abuse,' Maya said, 'and those weeks after, you internalised it and blamed yourself. You kept asking what could you have done better or differently. It was horrible to hear you and see you think this was somehow your fault.'

I explained to her – to myself, really – that this was in part because I could not fathom how a human like him existed. It was not in my frame of reference. While I could not understand him, I could understand myself and so I turned inward.

On the day of the clinic, and the days that followed, I would mostly mourn him. He was accomplished at putting himself at the centre of it all and this time was no different. 'You were grieving him,' Maya told me, and I was. Grieving the man I had allowed him to perform as being. The version of him I had failed to help, who had no choice but to punish me for my lack of success.

'I remember,' Maya said, 'saying that your body needs to focus on you right now, not him. I was really worried. All I could think was how the fuck do I get you through this. But there was something that stood out to me. You were taking the second batch of pills the doctor had given you for the abortion. And you were crying – and I said, "You need to look after your body right now, because you are about to pass this foetus and it's going to be hard, and your body really needs you right now." There was this point where the pain got so bad for you – you were on the floor, and you asked me for water. Then you asked me for fruit. Then you asked to watch a film. Then you asked for crackers. And for ice cream. And you weren't ashamed to say what you needed anymore.'

There is a point as a young girl where you are reminded not to ask. Told that to assert your needs is to be a nag, demanding, someone who is high maintenance. These were words for women who knew their own significance and worth, and as such became punishable for it. We watched our mothers and their mothers do it all, and ask nothing in return. And so, I was not simply asking Maya for a glass of water: I was telling her that I wanted to keep my body.

The codeine was strong enough to knock me out for a few hours. I was grateful for it. By midnight Maya had helped me into bed and taken my keys with the agreement that she would return in the morning to check on me. 'When I put you to bed, you were out of it. You were back asleep before I left. But when I came back the next day the latch was on the door.' She has recounted this story many times. I do not remember doing it. I do not understand how, as out of it as I was, I had found a way to get up and move. 'You put the latch on the door when you were practically passed out. I knew then that your instincts were there for you. Your response was to look after yourself. That's the moment I knew you were going to come out of this.'

A year on, Maya was eating and talking as if the last twelve months had been ten years or two days. 'We have to learn not to reward men for doing the things we do in a heartbeat for our friends. Even before we knew about the other women, when we were still trying to work out what had happened, all we could do was know then to stay away from men like this. He took no accountability. You physically carried all of that – in more ways than one – it was your body. And we can see him as this monster beyond our comprehension, but if you take him apart all of his traits are in the men that we know.'

What is scary about *him* is that he is a manifestation of them all. He's not a monster – because everything about him is what we know to be masculine-taught traits. Lying, cheating, using women for their homes, their bodies, not being a good father. All of this happens in smaller doses with other men.

Perhaps it's not been in one place quite like this – but we have seen all of his faces before.

★

We have seen all of his faces before.

The man who says he's working after hours, then you learn he was in the pub with an assistant from his office.

The man who lets you go home late alone, because he would rather stay out drinking with his friends than consider your safety.

The man who puts you down for chatting too much at the couples' dinner party, because you're too animated and embarrass yourself.

The man who says you're inappropriate when you talk too long to another guy.

The man who resents you having male friends.

The man who resents the time you spend with any friend.

The man who argues you're overreacting when he texts some girl he's just met in the middle of the night.

The man who expects you at his side for every important social event, but is never available for yours.

The man who diminishes your faith because he thinks all religion is dumb and you need to hear that.

The man who makes throwaway remarks about your race, who makes no effort to learn about it, as though he's not diminishing an inherent part of you.

The man who seeks reassurance but refuses you any.

The man who requires your advice but doesn't care for your concerns.

The man who doesn't listen when you talk about your promotion.

The man who undermines your work because his is more important.

The man who sneers at how much you earn.

The man who rolls his eyes when you get a new hobby.

The man who turns your music off because you have bad taste and he can't be expected to listen to this.

The man who insults how you look.

The man who tells you what to wear.

The man who suggests you should go on a diet. Who says you should exercise more.

The man who chooses his new kids over his older ones. Or his older ones over his new ones. Who spends money on his new girlfriend, but hasn't got any for his kid's school uniform.

The man who whispers that he wants to father your children when you've known him a week, then two years down the line says he's not sure he wants any, you shouldn't have taken him so seriously.

The man who laughs at jokes his pals make about whether that bruise on your arm was because you'd done something to get a little smack.

The man who turns his phone off when he'd made plans to meet you.

The man who bombards you with messages for a week, then goes quiet for a month.

The man who lets the dinner you've prepared go cold because he's having that one last drink.

The man who watches you clean the kitchen, the bathroom, do his washing, load the dishwasher because you're a woman and that's your job.

The man who sat just long enough through your abortion to feel and look like he'd done his part. If he even showed up at all.

The man who'll sleep with you regularly but isn't capable of committing right now.

The man who expects you to lower your expectations of a relationship because of his mental health crisis that he makes no attempt to help.

The man who asks you to wait for him, when he has no intention of coming back.

The man who cries, pleading for you to stay, when he knows you're ready to move on.

The man who insists you go on the pill because he doesn't like the feeling of condoms.

The man who judges how many sexual partners you've had. Or belittles you for your lack of experience.

The man who comes on too strong in bed and fails to acknowledge that his unwanted hand around your neck is a violation.

The man who expects you to give him a blow job because you're his girlfriend but doesn't apply the same logic to your own desires.

The man who thinks his time is more valuable than yours.

That he is more valuable than you.

★

The thing is, he was always gone. That began early on. Working after hours, and his phone turned off, and not raising his kids, and a clinic in Queens, and the comedy scene, and 'The Chain' is truly the most sensational song by Fleetwood Mac, perhaps in the world, and she sings, *If you don't love me now, you will never love me again* – because that's it, that's all there is, no more waiting – for him to be better, or come back, or change his mind, or be kinder, or stop cheating, stop lying, or see my worth, *if you don't love me now* – as I should be loved now . . .

. . . the thing is, he was always gone. That began early on. Hiding messages on his phone, and ignoring calls, and disappearing when you needed help, and 'The Chain' is the only song all of Fleetwood Mac created on an album they wrote when they were broken, pieced together from other songs they wrote separately that weren't (perhaps like everything) strong enough alone. The thing about being in a band with people you're in love with is one day it all ends, and you've got to sing your fucking way out of it, *if you don't love me now* . . .

. . . the thing is, he was always gone. That began early on. Grieving your baby alone, and raising your baby alone, and never giving you any money to help, and never giving you any time to help, and never giving you any help, and 'The Chain' is still the first song they play when they perform together, to remind each other how intrinsically linked they all are, *running in the shadows, damn your love, damn your lies* . . .

. . . the thing is, he was always gone. That began early on. Lying about where he is, and who he's with, and how he feels, and the thing about 'The Chain' is there's something remarkable about how she wrote those lyrics about him, and for forty years had him singing her own words back to her, *I can still hear you saying, you would never break . . .*

. . . the thing is, he was always gone, but it was never really about him anyway.

xi.

January 2018. East Village, New York.

The women are there, waiting when I walk in.

We hug each other. Compliment each other. I remember one woman's intricate black-lace gloves. Another woman's colourful patterned dress. I remember all of their faces, intelligent and beautiful and kind. We sit at a large table and go around it sharing our stories. No one speaks over anyone. No one cuts anyone off. Everyone is patient and caring, astonished by how cruel *he* had been to somebody else.

We walk a few blocks to another bar. We dance to Stevie Nicks's 'Edge of Seventeen'. We laugh. Buy a round of shots and raise a toast to each other. We take one selfie of us. Middle finger up to the camera.

*

December 2021. Dalston, London.

I read the menu. The seats are black leather, the decor comfortable. Exposed brickwork, low lighting,

the bottles lit up on the shelf behind the bar. I order
a glass of wine,
 and wait to meet the new women.

★

The thing is, *he* was always gone. That began early
on. Dying mothers, and agoraphobia, and a woman
had fallen with her baby in front of a train on the
subway, and a friend had killed his daughter and then
himself, and a cancelled flight, and a job in Zurich,
and silent friends, and wasn't the world spinning in
another direction from us, and a comedy show, and
a woman, so many women, and when dust clouds
break down, the substance at the centre will heat up,
and it is this, at the heart of the collapsing cloud, that
will one day become a star, and a stolen camera, and
hundreds of thousands gone, and *'The Chain' is truly
the most sensational song by Fleetwood Mac, perhaps in the
world*, and the blood on my bathroom walls, and the
snow, that fucking snow, and I – what was I? – *my love*,
when atoms of light elements are compressed under
enough stress to experience fusion, a star's life begins.

But this was never about me and *him*. It was about
me, and it was about *us*. I knew that when I learned
about the other women. Saw they were all brilliant,
and smart, and funny, quick-witted, and independent,
successful, and thoughtful, and loving, caring, and

compassionate. I realised then that I hadn't fallen for something, or someone, so wicked because I was deeply flawed or fucked up. Because I was naive. Because I was drunk. Because I was damaged. Because I deserved it. Rather – he had come after me, come after all of us, because we were everything he wished he was but knew he wasn't.

The only thing he ever got right is that he has excellent taste in women.

Women's powers were never mystical, nor are they fantastical. Our only magic is that, together, we survive.

Acknowledgements

My endless love, gratitude and thanks to the brave women in the chain, without whom there would be no book, or my own survival.

To the incredible team at W&N, who have championed this book from the start and have worked so very hard to protect the material, the women and me. In particular, my love and thanks to Jenny Lord, Francesca Pearce, Lily McIlwain, as well as Karen Rinaldi at Harper Collins USA. An extra huge thank you to my agent, Lisa Baker who has been both a friend and a source of strength throughout. Each of you has become a part of my chain in inexplicable ways.

Thank you to everyone who has helped me, helped the women in this book and helped the women in their own lives.

And finally to my parents: you have been my support system throughout my life and I can only hope to make you proud, in repayment of such a debt.

About the Author

CHIMENE SULEYMAN is a poet and writer of Turkish Cypriot descent who lives in London. She has written on the politics of race and immigration for the *Guardian*, the *Independent*, the BBC, NPR, and Sky News. She is the coeditor of *The Good Immigrant*.